THE FUTURE OF CAPITALISM AND ECONOMIC ANXIETIES

World Economic Changes In The Last Decades And The Future Of The World Financial System.

© Copyright 2020 by Franklin Jay Hackman

All rights reserved.

This document is geared towards providing exact and reliable information with regards to the topic and issue covered. The publication is sold with the idea that the publisher is not required to render accounting, officially permitted, or otherwise, qualified services. If advice is necessary, legal or professional, a practiced individual in the profession should be ordered.

- From a Declaration of Principles which was accepted and approved equally by a Committee of the American Bar Association and a Committee of Publishers and Associations.

In no way is it legal to reproduce, duplicate, or transmit any part of this document in either electronic means or in printed format. Recording of this publication is strictly prohibited and any storage of this document is not allowed unless with written permission from the publisher. All rights reserved.

The information provided herein is stated to be truthful and consistent, in that any liability, in terms of inattention or otherwise, by any usage or abuse of any policies, processes, or directions contained within is the solitary and utter responsibility of the recipient reader. Under no circumstances will any legal responsibility or blame be held against the publisher for any reparation, damages, or monetary loss due to the information herein, either directly or indirectly.

Respective authors own all copyrights not held by the publisher.

The information herein is offered for informational purposes solely, and is universal as so. The presentation of the information is without contract or any type of guarantee assurance.

The trademarks that are used are without any consent, and the publication of the trademark is without permission or backing by the trademark owner. All trademarks and brands within this book are for clarifying purposes only and are the owned by the owners themselves, not affiliated with this document

TABLE OF CONTENTS

1. Introduction 1
2. Globalization Of Financial Markets 5
3. Immigration And Globalization 39
4. World Economy Changes 67
5. China And Its Economic Muscles 85
6. Impacts Of The Emergency On The Creating And Change Nations 94
7. Today's America: A Land Of Broken Families And Few Prospects 127
8. What Future Difficulties Will Originators Face? 134

INTRODUCTION

Capitalism has experienced changes in the last centuries and has evolved into something new with complexities that need analyzation. In the current era, the economic system shows high turnovers due to political, social, technological, and business changes. These changes have brought confrontations between governments, and the powerful giant-tech companies bring a visual picture and an explanation to capitalisms involvements.

This outline considers the past, the present, and the eventual fate of financial turn of events. It starts with the conceptualization, definition, and estimation of monetary turn of events, featuring that a limited spotlight on the financial is lacking to catch improvement and even, incomprehensibly, monetary advancement itself. Key parts of financial and human improvement in the course of recent decades are then laid out, and the present scene is portrayed. The paper then thinks about the eventual fate of monetary turn of events, featuring the difficulties looked by creating nations, particularly the chances and dangers gave by the ongoing descending worldwide pattern in the portion of work in generally financial movement.

The conveyance of this rising salary among the populace is authentically in the area of monetary turn of events. Two key highlights of the dissemination of salary are disparity and destitution. If normal salary rises yet the imbalance of its appropriation likewise builds, then a libertarian point of view would write down the last as a negative part of financial turn of events. If neediness, the populace beneath a socially worthy degree of pay, additionally builds then this is another negative imprint to be set against rising normal pay in evaluating financial turn of events. Obviously, the genuine result on neediness will rely upon a cooperation between normal salary and imbalance and which of the two powers commands observationally.

If higher normal pay is joined by progressively inconsistent dispersion, a populist point of view will qualify it as negative. Developing destitution would likewise balance contrarily with higher normal pay in any assessment of financial turn of events

Be that as it may, identifying monetary advancement simply with salary is too tight an origination. Different parts of prosperity are without a doubt applicable. Instruction and wellbeing results, for instance, go past pay. They are significant markers of prosperity in their own right, however they impact, and are affected by, pay. High pay can convey an informed and solid populace, however an informed and sound populace additionally conveys high salary. In this way, any evaluation of advancement, and even monetary turn of events, needs to consider a more extensive scope of proportions of prosperity than just salary and its dispersion. Instruction and wellbeing, and their circulation in the populace, are significant also.

Dispersion isn't just about imbalance between people. Disparity across comprehensively characterized bunches is additionally a key factor. Sexual orientation disparity saps monetary advancement as it smothers the capability of a large portion of the populace. In this manner, upgrades in proportions of sexual orientation disparity are to be searched for in their own right, yet in addition in light of the commitments they make to financial development and to tending to monetary imbalance. Correspondingly, disparities among ethnic and territorial gatherings stir social pressure and influence the atmosphere for speculation and consequently financial development. It is difficult to isolate out these apparently non-financial measurements from the barely monetary. Monetary advancement is along these lines about improvement all the more for the most part.

A limited spotlight on allotted market pay misses on utilization of assets which are not evaluated fittingly in the market. The most significant of these is the earth, particularly with regards to ozone depleting substance outflows and environmental change. Rising national pay as traditionally estimated doesn't cost in the loss of indispensable natural assets at the national level nor, on account of environmental change, irreversible pushes toward calamitous dangers for the planet we live on.

A more extensive origination of improvement has been grasped by the worldwide network, first during that Time Advancement Objectives (MDGs) of 2000, and afterward through the Practical Advancement Objectives (SDGs) of 2015. The eight MDGs were extended and modified to seventeen SDGs, which incorporate traditional monetary estimates, for example, salary development and pay destitution, yet in addition imbalance, sex aberrations, and natural debasement (Kanbur, Patel, and Stiglitz, 2018). For sure, the crystallization and establishing of this more extensive conceptualization of improvement, and even of monetary turn of events, has been one of the definite advances during the previous decade of reasoning, and doubtlessly speaks to a push toward "another edification" in surveying directions of accomplishment. Yet, what have these directions been in the course of recent decades since World War II? The following segment takes up the story.

GLOBALIZATION OF FINANCIAL MARKETS

Indeed, even the most quick audit of significant universal monetary patterns in recent decades appears there have been progressive changes in world money related markets. During the 1950s and 1960s, budgetary organizations and their administrative structures in major modern nations advanced in relative separation from outer turns of events. During those years, most nations, including the US, forced limitations on worldwide capital developments. Significant worldwide institutional understandings after World War II, for example, the Bretton Woods understanding and the General Concession to Tariffs and Exchange, changed world exchange however did little to free the development of universal capital. After the money related interruptions of the 1930s, many had addressed whether free capital streams and changed capital markets were even alluring. In the Worldwide Money related Reserve, the essential commitment of part countries—their code of good conduct—was surrounded only as far as dodging limitations on current record installments. Such as installments for stock exchange, global administrations, speculation salaries and installments, settlements, and authority government moves. Then, the standards and the way of thinking as for capital exchanges were far different: numerous nations confined outward capital exchanges either because they favored their cash-flow to be contributed within their residential economies, or because they wished to forestall descending weight on their trade rates. Then, the standards of the capital exchanges and the way of thinking were far different: Many nations confined outward capital exchanges either because they favored their cash-flow to be contributed inside their residential economies or on the ground.

That circumstance and those perspectives changed significantly during the 1970s, and the pace of progress quickened in the 1980s. The cooperation of a few incredible powers has created gigantic capital streams across national limits. Simultaneously, the structure and activity of world budgetary markets have been changed. Today, world money related markets are exceptionally incorporated, and exchanges have gotten progressively unpredictable. These wonders are reflected in cross-posting of protections in a few nations, cross-country supporting and portfolio diversification, and 24-hour exchanging money related instruments at trades far and wide.

A large number of the channels utilized for money related exchanges have additionally changed. There has been a significant shift, moderately, from banks to nonbank monetary middle people, for example, financier houses, protections firms, insurance agencies, and annuity reserves. There has additionally been a shift from credits to protections and an ascent in the utilization of remote monetary focuses. Furthermore, there has been a flood in the utilization of new money-related instruments and, specifically, of subsidiary items (for example, budgetary alternatives, prospects, and swaps on financing costs, outside monetary forms, stocks, securities, and wares). These instruments are designed to address the issues and inclinations of different clients, remembering their longing to fence dangers for a domain of fluctuating trade rates, loan costs, stock costs, and item costs.

The extraordinary changes in world monetary markets have had significant ramifications for open strategy and information assortment. As a result of global capital developments, approaches, and advancements in different nations progressively impact residential monetary execution. As a result, there is a requirement for data about the new and rising worldwide money related condition. Nevertheless, changes that have occurred in world monetary markets themselves exacerbate the difficulty of gaining the data.

Given the difficulties in question and the budgetary requirements looked by measurable organizations in the open segment, a few inquiries emerge: What is the present requirement for information on universal capital exchanges? In what ways are present U.S. assortment frameworks satisfactory or insufficient? Are there reasonable blemishes.

A number of significant worldwide money related advancements have happened over the past 50 years, remembering the development of the Euromarkets for the mid-1960s, which bypassed household monetary guidelines. This report centers around changes in world capital markets related to money related deregulations in major modern nations since the late 1970s.

Sciences that ought to be adjusted? Are there elective approaches to accumulate the information that would be progressively precise, increasingly valuable, all the more opportune, all the more mechanically progressed, or less oppressive and expensive?

THE INVESTIGATION AND THE REPORT

With the assistance of the U.S. Financial Examination Department (BEA) Branch of Business, the Board on Worldwide Capital Exchanges was set up to look at the adjustments in the International monetary condition. Survey open and private requirements for information on global capital exchanges, audit the sufficiency of existing information, and also consider elective assortment strategies. Ensuing examination awards from the Central bank Board and the U.S. Branch of State likewise bolstered the investigation. The board's objective has been to create suggestions for the assortment of information on U.S. worldwide capital exchanges to help guarantee that the information are precise, opportune, significant, savvy, and valuable for dynamic in the years to come.

This examination is a follow-up to the one completed by a previous board of the Advisory Group on National Measurements. That report, Behind the Numbers: U.S. Exchange the World Economy (Kester, 1992), assessed the ampleness of information on U.S. stock exchange and worldwide administration exchanges. It prescribed strides to address the issues of underreporting of U.S. stock fares and insufficient inclusion of U.S. universal administration exchanges. It additionally proposed measures to improve checking of deals and buys by U.S. firms at home and abroad, just as those by outside firms in the US. It brought up that, of all U.S. worldwide exchanges (in merchandise, administrations, and capital streams), exchanges speaking to capital streams are the least satisfactorily archived. That report reasoned that improving the information on U.S. global capital exchanges would yield high adjustments, and this report tends to that issue.

Despite the fact that the changing worldwide exchange and the monetary condition has driven a few universal associations to attempt activities to improve the ideas and techniques for ordering global financial measurements, none of the subsequent investigations centers specifically around information on U.S. global capital exchanges. By and by, improving the nature of U.S. information would have significant ramifications for universal money related measurements. Better U.S. information would incredibly upgrade the convenience of data on worldwide capital streams, considering that the U.S. represents a huge.

Some portion of all universal exchanges. Different nations would likewise profit if improved U.S. measurements were accessible since U.S. exchanges include several other created and creating nations. The measurable issues of the U.S. information are also not exceptional. Refining U.S. information ideas, definitions, and strategies and orchestrating them with worldwide ones would advance global information likeness. Obviously, this improvement in likeness would also apply to the information from different nations. Information similarity is significant for global financial arrangement coordination, yet in addition to information trades between the US and various nations. The board accepts this report will add to a superior comprehension of the worldwide money related streams that have come to portray the quickly advancing global economy.

In leading this investigation, the board widely surveyed existing writing, including ongoing examinations by the

Universal Financial Store (1987, 1992b), the Central bank Board (Stekler, 1991; Stekler and Truman, 1992), and the Bank for Worldwide Settlements (1986, 1992a, 1992b). It analyzed the ideas, techniques, and methodology that U.S. government organizations use to gather information on worldwide capital exchanges, just as those utilized by other mechanical nations. It drew on the bits of knowledge and aptitude of numerous people in administrative offices, universal associations, remote government offices, organizations, exchange affiliations, and research associations, including those from the U.S. Division of Business, the U.S. Division of the Treasury, and the U.S. Central bank framework, just as the Worldwide Fiscal Store, the Bank for Universal Settlements, the Bank of Britain, the Bank of Japan, and the Deutsche Bundesbank. It con-fit specialists in the bookkeeping calling and other master bunches at present inspecting the progressions in worldwide money related markets and the treatment of complex budgetary exchanges. The board heard master declaration and looked into composed remarks from various government, scholastic, and industry clients on the ampleness of the current information. The board additionally solicited information filers from business and speculation banks, protections firms, financier houses, and global partnerships to become familiar with their perspectives on information announcing prerequisites.

In building up its suggestions, the board considered the current budgetary imperatives that face measurable organizations, just as the quickly developing world money related condition and the coming of inventive data and media communications advancements.

Bottom of Form

The remainder of this section audits the powers that have significantly changed world budgetary markets in the course of the most recent decade or thereabouts. Their suggestions for U.S. monetary and money related strategies portrays the current framework for accumulating information on U.S. global capital exchanges, taking note of its idea, inclusion, and strategies for collection. It examines the ampleness of the current framework, considering the perspectives on information assortment offices, information filers, and information clients, and makes proposals for improvements. It reviews the flood of exchanges in monetary subordinates and discusses about their suggestions for the inclusion and understanding of existing information on U.S. universal capital exchanges. 5 investigates the attainability of utilizing elective information sources and assortment strategies to improve the inclusion and precision of existing information, including robotization, the utilization of worldwide caretakers, trades, settlement, clearing houses, and databases of global associations.

Elements Adding To Globalization

The fast development and coordination of world monetary markets since the late 1970s can be credited to a few elements. They incorporate an overall push toward deregulation of money related establishments and exchanges; macroeconomic irregular characteristics among nations, which have incited capital streams; improved information about the market and monetary conditions the world over. The achievements in data and correspondences innovation that have expanded the limit exponentially with respect to taking care of enormous volumes of budgetary exchanges while significantly diminishing unit exchange expenses and utilizing new money related instruments. Moreover, a rivalry has developed among different kinds of budgetary foundations in different nations, whose portfolio the executive's methodologies in unpredictable markets have brought about new items and new methods of activity. This improvement in world budgetary markets in the light of these powers and the U.S. experience can be followed back around two decades.

Deregulation And Advancement Of Budgetary Exercises

The pattern toward money-related deregulation quickened in the mid-1970s when the administration controls on budgetary exercises that had been built up during the 1950s and 1960s proved ineffective and caused genuine wasteful aspects of capital allocation and fiscal arrangement activity. The US expelled its last capital controls in 1973; Germany significantly diminished its limitations on capital developments during the 1970s; and the Unified Realm disassembled its trade controls in 1979, Japan in the mid-1980s, and France and Italy in the late 1980s. Nations grasped deregulation as it was expected that free capital progressions would open up both sparing and venture open doors for firms and people and better match the changing needs of providers and clients of assets, thus encouraging the proficient capital distribution and advancing pay and yield development.

The procedure of incorporation has additionally intensified as outside speculators and money related organizations have been permitted moderately openly to enter residential markets in different pieces of the world. For example, the number of outside banks in the U.S. rose from around 122 to 280 somewhere within the range of 1978 and 1991. Branches and organizations of outside banks held total resources of $626 billion in 1991, up from $90 billion out of 1978. In 1991, remote banks represented 18 percent of absolute financial resources in this nation and worked 565 workplaces (Central bank Leading body of Governors, 1993:1).4 Then, at the hour of the "enormous detonation" of 1986—the deregulation of protections showcases in the Unified Realm—numerous U.S. protections firms and banks extended their quality in London through acquisitions and different methods. There are different proportions of an expanded mix of money related markets. Over the equivalent 1978-1991 period, the estimation of U.S. resources abroad rose more than three-overlap while the estimation of outside resources in the U.S. indicated a considerably progressively emotional six-overlay increment.

MACROECONOMIC CONDITIONS

In a domain of deregulated and changed money related markets, universal capital developments have been driven basically by financial essentials. The macroeconomic states of different nations and their exchange and duty arrangements, for instance, influence the normal paces of profit for different interests in different markets. In the mid-to-late 1970s, enormous capital streams came about as a result of the reusing of oil send out surpluses of the Association of Oil Trading Nations. A large number of them through worldwide banks to sovereign borrowers in creating nations. In the late 1970s and mid-1980s, there was an extensive capital departure from many creating nations as uncompetitive loan fees and trade rates, enormous financial shortages, and high

4   Foreign keeps money with U.S. branches, and offices originally got subject to government guidelines with the appropriation of the Global Financial Demonstration of 1978. Extra administrative authority was given by the Outside Bank Supervision Upgrade Act in 1991.

Outside obligation loads caused significant damage to those nations. Starting in the mid-1980s, huge capital inflows into the US were a significant wellspring of financing for the sizable government spending shortfalls being caused.

Differences in the blend of financial and money related arrangements between the US and other modern nations over the previous decade have straightforwardly influenced trade rates for the dollar. The enormous developments of the dollar against other significant monetary forms since the 1980s, this way, have added to increments in deals and acquisition of dollar-named protections and the extension of remote money exchanging.

In 1992, differentials moving toward 6 rate focuses or more in loan fees between the US and Germany pulled in cash-flow to Germany from the US (and different nations). Following unification, Germany depended on high loan costs to hose inflationary weights emerging from the tremendous expenses of rejuvenating the economy of previous East Germany. Additionally in the mid-1990s, fast monetary development in East Asian nations and huge fare surpluses in those nations have created pools of reserve funds that stream into the worldwide economy to back the ventures that offer the most noteworthy paces of return.

Mechanical Advancements

Innovation is another power that has changed the activity and structure of global money related markets. Innovations in data and media interaction have significantly enhanced the preparation and dispersal of data. Around the globe, the participants of the showcase are assaulted with a plenty of data. And an uproar of emotions, reports, and gossipy tidbits, some of which is imparted by PCs.

Moreover, the electronic exchange has allowed requests to move across landmasses, legitimately from clients to specialists and sellers. Robotized exchange executive.

One case of such frameworks is GLOBEX, an electronic exchanging framework propelled by the Chicago Commercial Trade and the Chicago Leading body of Exchange combination with Reuter, the English data benefits firm. Key U.S. government protections and remote trade are exchanged in worldwide markets. Nonstop exchanging is extending because it speeds up and power over the bearing of data streams, and can bring about huge benefits or decreased misfortunes in money-related markets. The more noteworthy straightforwardness with which monetary merchants can access different markets and their decreased expenses have empowered them to exploit even little overall revenues around the globe.

Moreover, communications among business sectors, which have been encouraged by mechanical developments, have given market members chances to diversify, fence, and increment benefits on their ventures, accordingly advancing the utilization of new money-related items and instruments. In recent years, there has been a fast development in budgetary subsidiaries, for example, advances, prospects, alternatives, swaps, and complex mixes of them on financing costs, trade rates, stocks, and securities. The main role of these instruments is to support introduction against the hazard, and many are exchanged across fringes. Going with this ascent in subordinates has been the quick extension of over-the-counter markets that include exchanging over PC arranges in protections custom fitted to the specific needs of individual financial specialists, borrowers, and middle people.

Rivalry AMONG Money Related AND NONFINANCIAL Organizations

Facilitating capital controls, advancing monetary markets, and mechanical developments have intensified rivalry among budgetary and nonfinancial foundations in different nations. This has, therefore, changed the structure of world budgetary markets.

In recent years, an outstanding advancement in the universal fund has been the development of securitization—a procedure of changing over resources that would typically fill in as guarantee for a bank credit into protections that are increasingly fluid and can be exchanged at a lower cost than the hidden resource. This procedure has been cultivated, in addition to other things, by mechanical advancements. With PCs and electronic record-keeping, budgetary foundations can inexpensively package together with an arrangement of advances (initially, contract advances) with little categories, gather the intrigue and principle buddy installments, and offer the cases to these installments to an outsider as security. This procedure of pooling advances and selling protections supported by the advances has been seen by money related foundations as more productive than customary financing through monetary delegates in specific circumstances, and it has been utilized, for instance, for car advances and charge card commitments.

In a situation of deregulation, nonbank budgetary organizations have conceived new and different approaches to move cash from savers to borrowers. Lately, in the US, for instance, benefits reserves, currency advertise assets, and insurance agencies, among others, have progressively attracted investment funds from bank stores. Thus, these institutional speculators, which are preferred capable over people to get the required data for the outside venture, have intensely put resources into remote protections, cultivating the fast extension of universal security and value markets.5 Under these conditions, there now are differing foundations contending to offer money related types of assistance; protections have become an inexorably significant component in global capital streams.

In the interim, global enterprises that produce and sell products and ventures on a worldwide scale look for overall hotspots for their financing and speculation needs. To serve these customers, monetary foundations have diversified the administrations they offer, among which exchanges are in remote trade, currency showcase instruments, and subordinate items, all on an overall scale. These complex monetary instruments permit financial specialists a variety of options for supporting and shifting dangers, which, at an expense, can give more noteworthy conviction of worldwide receipts and installments, or, at times, for taking on presentation with an exceptionally utilized position. There is a huge market for such instruments in the present condition, as universal organizations, examiners, and financial specialists are confronted with unstable trade rates, loan costs, and ware costs.

Over the previous decade, business paper exceptional developed at a normal yearly pace of around 17 percent. In 1988 the size of the business paper advertised even briefly outperformed that of the market in U.S. Treasury bills. The guarantors of business paper in the US have included outside companies and remote money related establishments. As indicated by the Central bank study (Post, 1992), business paper will stay a significant wellspring of momentary assets for organizations during the 1990s. High-appraised outside enterprises in the US, pulled in by the liquidity and the ease of the market, are probably going to be among the new guarantors.

While remote enterprises have been bringing capital up in the US, outside money-related utilization focuses by U.S. organizations has additionally been broad. The Central Bank of New York (1992a) gauges that advances to U.S. business and mechanical organizations that started seaward rose from $37 billion out of 1983 to $174 billion before the finish of 1991. Seaward bank advances to U.S. organizations flooded during the 1980s as remote banks benefited themselves of the chance to keep away from the hold cost of making credits in the Unified States.8 The quickest development in these seaward advances to U.S. business and modern organizations has happened in the Cayman Islands and mechanical nations, Japan as a typical example.

In this serious condition, banking exercises have likewise significantly changed. During the late 1970s and the mid-1980s, enormous business banks in numerous nations, incorporating those in the U.S, looked to help their benefits by loaning huge entireties to creating nations. From that point forward, even though store taking and loaning have remained the center business of business banks, an expanding segment of their pay has originated from sources other than the differentials between the premium they pay on stores and the premium they charge on credits. To improve net revenues, notwithstanding offering expense paying business warning administrations, banks have progressively bundled resources not generally exchanged, (for example, contract advances, vehicle advances, corporate receivables, and Visa receivables) into tradable protections. They likewise have gone to subordinate instruments as circumstances have declined in customary interbank store markets.9 Banks have additionally sought after off-

The development of seaward credits declined after the Central bank evacuated the significant save necessities in 1990.

The sharp reduction in interbank business has been credited to the low returns and possibly huge counterparty dangers identified with this sort of business (Bank for Universal Settlements, 1992a).

Report exercises to shift resources off their monetary records and in this manner improve their capital proportions. At present, an expanding extent of banks' credit and liquidity exposures has been acquired off their accounting reports (see Section 4). With the development of nonbank money-related establishments, banks have additionally offered reinforcement credit extensions or certifications to these foundations, for instance, the support of business paper issues. Under the 1988 Basle Capital Accord, banks' suggested capital prerequisites for these exercises are a lot of lower than for ordinary loans.10 One significant job that enormous business banks have held is to give installments and clearing instruments to most budgetary exchanges.

Another improvement in the structure of world monetary markets is that with the rise in the use of subsidiary instruments by both bank and nonbank budgetary foundations, protections, advances, prospects, and alternatives markets have gotten progressively connected. Advances in broadcast communications advances enabled collaborations within these business sectors.

Arrangement ISSUES Emerging FROM GLOBALIZATION

A few advantages have been refered to because of the adjustments in the structure and activity of worldwide monetary markets. Capital versatility and money related developments are credited with having given savers and borrowers a more extensive scope of venture choices and simpler and less expensive access to outside financing. They are additionally accepted to have encouraged more prominent diversification of portfolios and expanded the size of business sectors. The internationalization of capital markets is said to have encouraged the financing of worldwide installments lopsided characteristics and supported increasingly effective allotment of worldwide assets.

In any case, there has also been an across the board observation that deregulation, globalization, and money-related advancements have convoluted the detailing and implementation of financial and monetary approaches, prompted more prominent instability in budgetary markets, and presented new and profoundly complex components of hazard that can

The Basle Capital Accord alludes to the base capital guidelines consented to by the Basle Advisory group on Banking Supervision for the supervision of universal financial gatherings and their cross-fringe foundations. The Basle Board of trustees is comprised of the financial directors of the Gathering of Ten mechanical nations and Luxembourg. The 1988 accord required a base 8-percent proportion of a bank's cash-flow to its hazard weighted presentation to credit chance, which was to be achieved before the finish of 1992. Proposition for capital measures covering market dangers are being talked about because of the significant disturbances in global monetary frameworks. Global capital versatility not just has prompted developing linkages of world money related markets, yet additionally has expanded the degree to which macroeconomic arrangements and economic situations of one nation can significantly influence those of others. In the interim, the securitization of exchanges and development in the utilization of money related subsidiary instruments have made worldwide budgetary streams progressively perplexing and less straightforward, entangling supervision of monetary establishments. This segment talks about a few parts of the impact of new worldwide real factors in budgetary markets on a country's monetary approaches and money related oversight.

Macroeconomic Strategies

Financing costs and the accessibility of capital in a mechanical nation are presently considerably more affected than in the past by loan costs and credit accessibility in different nations. An end product is that money-related (and financial) improvements in a significant mechanical nation have greater macroeconomic impacts on different nations than they did when the capital was less portable globally. A clear model was the impact in 1992 of high loan costs in Germany on different individuals from the European Fiscal Framework, as well as on other mechanical nations, including the US. The more liberated progression of-assets among nations doesn't really carry their loan fees into line with each other. Financing costs may differ among nations when there exists a desire for trade rates to change or when there is a premium identified with different kinds of hazards. Regardless, an adjustment in loan costs in a significant modern nation can unequivocally influence both financing costs and trade rates in different nations.

The development in cross-outskirt stores additionally has suggestions for financial approaches. At a point when cross-outskirt stores were little and generally steady, they could be disregarded while looking at the conduct of residential money related totals. As of late as possible, development in these stores has added to inquiries regarding the value of money-related totals as markers of the snugness or slack of U.S. money-related conditions, to a limited extent since proportions of U.S. financial totals do not fully catch stores held by U.S. inhabitants in banks situated in remote countries.11 In

The three significant measures are M1, M2, and M3. M1

incorporates money outside the Treasury Office, Central bank banks, and the vaults of safe organizations; explorer's checks of nonbank backers; request stores at all business expansion, as a result of remote contributions of dollar-named commitments, net U.S. global capital streams don't completely show trade advertise pressures on the dollar (Cooper, 1986).

Besides, it is contended that under gliding trade rates, expanded worldwide capital portability can animate the speed with which tight money related strategies moderate expansion since monetary standards will, in general, acknowledge because of higher loan fees. The bizarre speed of the U.S. disinflation in the mid-1980s is a model (Willett and Wihlborg, 1990).

Upgraded capital versatility also influences financial strategy. Previously, when a nation's monetary arrangement prompted an enormous spending deficiency, the impact was principally residential, with the progressively fast development of national pay and yield and perhaps at the same time in some swarming out of private venture as the administration obtained more and financing costs rose. A present, a significant outcome could be a huge exchange shortfall, if high loan fees are levied on foreign assets and the conversion scale increases in value. This marvel was obvious in the US during the 1980s when enormous government spending shortages were joined by huge exchange

risen on the grounds that institutional financial specialists and other expert cash directors can move huge pools of investment funds abroad. They progressively do so when they ascertain they can acquire higher paces of return, in the wake of considering trade chance

Surveying The Steadiness Of Budgetary Markets

As assets move all the more effectively and all the more promptly starting with one nation then onto the next, the costs of budgetary instruments (for instance, protections and outside trade) might be dependent upon more noteworthy unpredictability. Progressively, trade rates (the costs of remote trade) are influenced by "news"— the progression of new data—and by the desires it causes. The costs of bonds and stocks are likewise affected. Also, trade rates and protections costs communicate with one another. Subsequently, protections costs in a single nation would now be able to be influenced by the conduct of remote just as local moneylenders and financial specialists, even though the level of impact differs starting with one circumstance then onto the next, contingent upon an assortment of conditions. Subsequently, when the U.S. securities exchange declined strongly in October 1987, there were overall impacts. However, the huge drop in the costs of Japanese stocks in 1991-1992 had a minimal recognizable effect on financial exchanges in the U.S. and different nations.

On a fundamental level, upgraded capital versatility could lead to more stable markets rather than higher prominent instability of protection costs and trade rates, as it makes showcases less "flimsy" as far as quantities of members and potential progressions of assets. Regardless, the data insurgency, which has expanded commonality with monetary, money-related, and political conditions the world over and along these lines supported universal loaning and contributing, additionally brings a consistent progression of news that can make banks and financial specialists roll out unexpected improvements in their property in their own and different nations. In this manner, markets are powerless against bigger swings—both in the short and medium-term—in a universe of incorporated money related markets and huge overall liquidity.

12 The value elements made by subordinate instruments can likewise worsen this potential. In remote trade markets, such swings in costs have driven on occasion to facilitated intercession by national banks planned for hosing the short-and medium-term instability of trade rates. Since the gathering of seven fund clergymen and national bank governors in the Louver in February 1987, the financial experts of those nations have endeavored to keep up their trade rates within expansive reaches.

The huge volume of assets streaming across national limits, starting from one money to the next, poses a risk that a breakdown in one monetary framework could spread throughout the World. The October 1987 U.S. Securities Exchange Crash showed the speed with which major monetary stuns can resonate across worldwide markets, and it caused to notice the kinds of liquidity, repayment, and freedom issues that can emerge in cash and value markets.13 Many budgetary delegates are receiving and sending incredibly huge aggregates, compared to their capital and fluid resources, through installment systems. To make the necessary installments, they are subject to receipts from others. If one middle person in the installments component becomes incapable, out of the blue, of making the installments for which it is at risk and others won't loan to it, issues for different establishments and in different focuses can grow rapidly.

In the business banking framework, national banks have,

for quite some time, been set up to go about as loan specialists after all other options have run out to empower banks to adapt to liquidity issues. The bank assessment process additionally plans to make preparations for indebtedness in business banks, and there is a close global collaboration among chiefs of business banks, who meet routinely at the Bank for Universal Repayments at Basle. However, there are inquiries concerning whether nonbank monetary middle people—including specialists and vendors and speculation banks—are similarly very much regulated and, if these nonbank foundations are sufficiently managed, regardless of whether national banks ought to likewise go about as their loan specialists of last resort.14

13 There have been a few activities in the US and abroad to improve the clearing and settlement frameworks from that point forward.

14 The Specialized Board of the Global Association of Protections Commissions has made progress in the direction of worldwide hazard-based capital sufficiency principles for protections firms. Endeavors are being made in order to accommodate the differences between the capital necessities material to nonbank protections firms and those relevant to banks that take part in protection exercises. In the U.S, Congress, as of late, gave power to the Product Prospects Exchanging Commission to share data more fully and to help out outside controllers. Furthermore, the Protections and Trade Commission is considering changing the U.S. protections firms' capital gauges to perceive progressively outside business sectors. And to also gather information important to survey the requirement for extra guidelines of the budgetary

exercises of U.S. protections firms' unregulated associates and representative vendor holding organizations.

National banks and monetary controllers were also concerned about the hazard introduction of members participating in the exchanges of subsidiaries. Dangers are presented from various perspectives, including the unpredictability of the basic markets. A market member's presentation may radically change with a vacillation in loan costs or value costs: a slight shift in share costs, for instance, may lead to a major change in the estimation of a stock-record alternative. Different dangers relate to the administration of sizable situations by huge money related foundations and the credit nature of these "discount" ventures and their clients. Still, another hazard concerns illiquidity. Although subsidiaries exchanged on trades have numerous purchasers and merchants, those custom-made to specific clients' needs (for example, those exchanged the over-the-counter markets) are increasingly difficult to sell, as they are increasingly difficult to value and to support against trade.

Furthermore, the darkness of a portion of these exchanges, particularly over-the-counter agreements, aggravates the difficulty for controllers of observing business sector members in subordinates. Moreover, as more and bigger dealers, driven by specialized exchanging techniques, look to move progressively enormous entireties between business sectors, showcase unpredictability is probably going to increment. The closer linkages among business sectors that are encouraged by the development of subsidiaries imply that money-related stuns can be transmitted across business sectors rapidly.

The development in subsidiary instruments has made not

just complex chains of counterparty (purchaser or dealer) exposures yet, also, on account of conversion scale gets a significant extension of global installment and settlement exercises. To decrease dangers and guard against installment "gridlock," the Central bank and other national banks are intently observing their installment and settlement instruments. Likewise, the Basle Board has concentrated on methods for growing the Basle Capital Accord to cover credit chance and different kinds of market dangers, for example, remote conversion standard hazard, loan cost hazard, and position chances in exchanged value protections. (For a conversation of the different sorts of dangers emerging from subsidiaries exchanges, see Central bank Leading body of Governors et al., 1993; Bank for Universal Settlements, 1992b; Gathering of Thirty, 1993).

Generally, the cooperation between nations' loan fees, trade rates, and protection costs, hurried by the expansion in capital portability and the linkages of world budgetary markets, has given rise to significant approaches. The monetary presentation of one nation—particularly a mechanical one with high capital versatility—will be influenced by approaches and market improvements in other country attempts. There is an obscuring of the customary differentiation among residential and global monetary arrangements. Strategy creators in major modern nations need to assess strategies and arrangement expectations somewhere else. In a universe of developing associations among countries, improved capital versatility will help strategy creators accomplish their local macroeconomic targets; in different cases, it might undermine the impact of national strategies on household financial execution. In this new worldwide monetary condition, to all the more likely plan U.S. macroeconomic arrangement, screen monetary market execution, and manage the steadiness of the household money related framework, far reaching data on U.S. worldwide capital exchanges will be required. At the same time, unusual changes in the world's money-related markets have reduced the viability of customary information assortment techniques and the sufficiency of the current information. This segment gives an outline and a few instances of the lack of current information. The rest of the report. Progressively significant, as discussed above, internationalization of budgetary exchanges has offered to ascend strategy worries about the liquidity, dissolvability, and dependability of the U.S. money-related framework to the extent that it is influenced by outside business sectors. These are issues for which the equalization of-installments structure was not intended to treat. There is have to enhance the current offset of-installments information with tends exchanges other data on U.S. budgetary exercises need to be enhanced to manage the choices to be made on bunch rising open approaches.

In its report (Kester, 1992), the Board on Remote Exchange Insights suggested enhancing the current exchange measurements, gathered under the parity of-installments system, with monetary data gathered outside it to all the more likely delineate the globalized U.S. business exercises in merchandise and enterprises. Such a more extensive structure would make an extraordinary contribution to addressing issues such as U.S. worldwide seriousness and the effect of outside exchange and direct speculation on U.S. business and creation. This report makes suggestions to improve the inclusion and precision of the current information, yet it also proposes approaches to enhance them with information on the blossoming money-related subordinates exchanges gathered outside the conventional equalization of-installments structure.

The requirement for improved information is additionally proved by the fragmented bookkeeping of the sizable U.S. worldwide capital streams as of late and the vulnerability related to it about the U.S. money related situation on the planet economy and other monetary and budgetary turns of events. A couple of models follow.

- U.S. insights for 1982 demonstrate that the rate at which out-of-state people were getting resources in the U.S. was not exactly the same rate at which U.S. inhabitants were making sure about resources abroad. Be that as it may, the factual error of the U.S. balance-of-installments accounts in that year was bigger than the difference between these two aggregates: current record receipts or net capital inflows of approximately about $41 billion were not identified or recorded. Along these lines, the course of the net capital stream could have been something contrary to what was announced in the 1982 U.S. balance-of-installments accounts.

- When at first discharged, information for 1985 on the U.S. net global venture position demonstrated that remote resources of U.S. inhabitants were not exactly their liabilities to outsiders. The press alluded to the U.S. as being "an account holder country" just because since before World War I. The cumulating liabilities, whose weight could fall on the cutting edge also, were esteemed to infer the commitment to pay the future premium, profits, benefits, and amortization to outside financial specialists. Be that as it may, the U.S. information on U.S. occupants' immediate speculations and claims on outsiders was recorded at book esteem, overlooking any expansion in advertise estimation of the venture after some time. A few investigators accepted that this wellspring of modest representation of the truth in the U.S. global speculation position was enormous to such an extent that U.S. liabilities to outsiders for 1985 were, truth be told, littler than U.S. property of remote resources. However, others called attention to an estimation blunder the other way: the aggregate measurable inconsistency in the U.S. balance-of-installments accounts as announced simultaneously totaled $117 billion for the years 1981-1985 alone, showing potentially sizable unreported capital inflows.

In this way, this information has experienced a few corrections, and BEA has started to distribute an incentive on the market just as recorded quotes of absolute resource esteem. As for late-distributed information (Agency of Monetary Investigation, 1994a:71), remote resources claimed by U.S. inhabitants in 1985 surpassed outsiders' responsibility for. Resources estimated either by chronicled cost or market esteem. Since 1989, in any case, outsiders' responsibility for. Resources have surpassed the outside possessions of U.S. occupants, using either the verifiable expense or market esteem measures.

Indeed, even up-to-date information may keep an eye on outsiders' interests more closely in the US than on U.S. occupants' foreign ventures, whatever they may be. Until 1994, U.S. possessions of remote protection had not been thoroughly reviewed since World War II.15 Moreover, despite the recorded "net obligation," official measurements show that U.S. income (premium and benefits) on speculation abroad continues to be greater than the profit paid by the U.S. to outsiders on their U.S. ventures..

- Until the 1980s, as noted above, banks commanded the global money related framework, yet securitization has happened quickly from that point forward. U.S. official insights show remote acquisition of U.S. protections as surpassing bank-announced liabilities as the biggest part of the capital inflow in 1985. In any case, an ongoing report by the Central Bank of New York (1992a) shows that as much as $70 billion of remote loaning to U.S. businesses that occurred seaward during the 1980s was excluded from the official measurements of U.S. worldwide capital exchanges. This subsidization brings up the question of whether official measurements have exaggerated protection as a source of funding and downplayed the significant job despite everything played by banks.16

- U.S. insights show that 1985 deals of U.S. Treasury protections to outsiders, albeit commonly more prominent than those in 1980, were still generally little ($20.5 billion, of which 83 percent was offered to Japanese inhabitants) (Frankel, 1988:592). However, official Japanese insights show that the estimation of

U.S. Treasury protections purchased by Japanese occupants was a lot bigger than was appeared in the U.S. information. For 1986, the inconsistency between the U.S.- revealed deals of U.S. Treasury protections to Japan and Japanese-detailed acquisition of U.S. Treasury protections was $37 billion ($12.8 billion and $49.4 billion, separately). Since U.S. Treasury protections are sold in worldwide markets and the U.S. official information, don't identify a definitive proprietor of the protections, the property of U.S.

- The review was directed in 1994, however, as of mid-1994 there was no firm calendar for information discharge.

- Recently distributed reexamined information (Department of Monetary Investigation, 1994a) contain sensational upward corrections in appraisals of U.S. nonbanks liabilities to outsiders for the years 1983-1993. These updates result from the BEA proceeding with the program to utilize information revealed by remote banks. Much of the update depends on information from the Bank for Global Settlements (BIS) on bank claims detailed in the Caribbean and Asian financial focuses.

- Protections held by specific nations stay muddled. Also, U.S. information on capital exchanges doesn't identify the degree to which U.S. resources held by outsiders are by and by supported in remote monetary forms. This insufficiency has hindered the examination of the dollar's powerlessness in remote portfolio shifts.

- The US had the option to keep financing enormous exchange deficiencies 1987 and from there on without significant devaluation of the dollar: one clarification is that remote national banks stepped in to purchase dollars when private speculators had gotten careful about exchanging. Albeit official insights on national bank exchanges are accepted to be better than those on private exchanges, even the official measurements are tricky. At the point when an outside national bank obtains dollars and stores them in a business bank abroad, the dollar possessions won't appear in the U.S. measurements as authentic outside possessions of dollars. They will show up as U.S. liabilities to outside business banks. The distributed figures of remote authority possessions of dollars, along these lines, may downplay the degree of outside government intercession in outside trade showcases; this occurred in 1987. The Central Bank of New York, utilizing its information and different sources, has assessed that outside authentic acquisition of dollars in 1987, including the private diverting of legitimate capital, may have been right around multiple times higher than the $45 billion that was recorded in the U.S. balance-of-installments accounts.

- In the late 1980s, Americans were increasingly worried about another sizable part of the capital inflow: outside direct interest in the US. News media reported that Japanese and other remote financial specialists were building manufacturing plants and purchasing resources in the US, including such national images as

Rockefeller Center and the Seattle Sailors baseball crew. How broad is a remote direct interest in the US, and what is its monetary effect? The accessibility of information bearing on these inquiries has extended over the last few years, yet holes remain (see Part 3).

- In 1990 and 1991, with the American economy in a downturn, an investigation emerged as to whether the financial strategy was excessively tight. During 1990, M1 developed at 4.0 percent, and it developed 8.7 percent in 1991. This may have seemed, by all accounts, to be sufficient cash development to back the economy. In 1990, be that as it may, an expansion in cash extraordinary comprised 75% of the increment in M1 ($24.2 billion of $32.0 billion). A few evaluations recommend that over a portion of U.S. dollar cash extraordinary is held in Latin America and other outside nations.

GLOBALIZATION OF BALANCES frequently a decent haven from neighborhood expansion and tax collection. A Central bank examination proposes that there was an enormous unmeasured outpouring of U.S. money in 1990 (maybe $15 billion of the $47.4 billion blunders and exclusions in the U.S. global exchange accounts 17). As a result, the observed M1 developments have provided a misleadingly expansionary sign of financial conditions (Stekler and Truman, 1992:5). In 1991, cash expansion clarified only 28 percent of the increase in M1 ($20.5 billion, $72.0 billion). Indisputably, better information on U.S. universal cash shipments would assist the Central Bank in designing financial arrangements for the objectives it seeks to achieve.

Economies are developing due to increases in the creation of products and enterprises. Monetary development can be the result of purchaser spending, universal exchange, and business speculation.

Times of development has occurred since the beginning to a limited extent due to new revelations, such as shale oil in the 2000s, making the U.S. one of the world's top oil producers. The web approach brought new advances, the internet business, and transformed the way the business was done.

In any case, developments and innovative advances could not have taken place without capital speculation, which involves purchases and ventures by organizations and financial specialists to make a more splendid monetary future.

Clarifying Monetary Development

Monetary development in the U.S. is principally determined by buyer spending and capital spending from organizations. As shoppers purchase more homes, for instance, home development and temporary workers see increments in income. As organizations put resources into their business to extend their items and administrations, they enlist more workers and increment pay rates or wages. The entirety of the action prompts financial development as estimated by GDP or Gross domestic product—the all-out yield of merchandise and enterprises for a country in a given period.

How Capital Venture Identifies with Monetary Development

Capital venture results when organizations buy capital merchandise. Capital merchandise incorporates resources, for example, processing plants, machines, PCs, vehicles, apparatuses, and other creation hardware. Capital speculations are long haul in nature that enables organizations to generate income for a long time by including or improving the creation of offices and boosting operational effectiveness.

Extra or improved capital merchandise expands the profitability of work, making organizations increasingly profitable and effective. More up-to-date hardware or industrial facilities could prompt the creation of more items at a faster rate. In addition, another creation office may use less power due to new hardware and a vitality-effective structure. Therefore, the organization's benefits increment due to more items being created at a lower cost and faster turnaround times.

A business does not see a rapid increase in income when it creates capital products. In order to make it monetarily feasible to increase or improve the capital structure, an organization must have satisfactory money or financing through an obligation (securities) or value — stock to raise reserves.

Expanded capital speculation takes into consideration more innovative work in the capital structure. This extending capital structure raises the beneficial effectiveness of work. As work turns out to be increasingly effective, the expanded productivity across the nation leads to financial development for the whole nation or higher total national output.

Capital products are not equivalent to budgetary capital or human capital. Budgetary capital incorporates the assets important for the continuation and growth of a business, either by obligation or value, and human capital speaks to human work or laborers. It requires monetary money to put resources into capital merchandise while, at the same time, it takes human cash-flows to configuration, manufacturing, and working capital products.

KEY TAKEAWAYS

- Capital venture is when organizations buy capital merchandise, for example, industrial facilities, machines, PCs, vehicles, and creation gear.

- U.S. financial development is principally determined by buyer spending and business venture spending.

- Capital venture can be a differentiating factor in whether the U.S. posts a solid development rate or a weak development rate.

IMMIGRATION AND GLOBALIZATION

The universal movement of individuals lies at the center of the progressing procedure of globalization. Individuals move to improve their financial possibilities, guarantee a progressively secure living condition, re-join with their relatives, or evade mistreatment in their nation of beginning. These among different reasons inspired the 3% of the total populace who wound up on a universal relocation direction in 2005. Since an enormous extent of vagrants head towards created nations, the portion of global transients in these nations came to as much as 9.5% in 2005.1 These individuals experience not just significant financial and social outcomes of their turn, yet in addition mental ones. Relocation may include a new position with more significant compensation, losing old and setting up new social ties, just as mental expenses of missing the country. Relocation, be that as it may, doesn't just influence the destiny of the individuals who are legitimately included. Different impacts rise at the interface of transient and local populaces. Migrants may carry with them new societies or inclinations, vie for specific employments and make others, or guarantee openly financed government disability benefits. All the more extensively, transients add to a progressively proficient designation of assets and frequently become a main thrust of information move and mechanical headway. Every one of these impacts have repercussions for the local populace, who may respond to transient inflows with respect to their present activity, yet in addition to long haul speculation plans, for example, those concerning training. At long last, locals may see workers decidedly or contrarily and structure their mentalities appropriately. Relocation is a unique wonder including numerous exciting bends in the road. Driven by a huge number of potential reasons, vagrants may move briefly or forever, transnationally and broadly, exclusively or in gatherings, come back to their nations of starting point or move to another nation, or move between at least two nations in a round manner. The complex fundamental procedures driving movement and its belongings have pulled in a significant and developing consideration of researchers. Chiswick (1978) and Borjas (1985) spearheaded scientific work on outsider change in have social orders. This writing features the significance of involvement with the host nation and stresses the significance of companion impacts, nation of beginning, religion, training, just as various segment qualities, for example, age and sexual orientation. From a different point of view, the investigation of the relocation choice has been enlivened and progressed by Harris and Todaro (1970), Becker (1964), Mincer (1978), and Borjas (1985). Outsider self-choice talked about by Borjas (1987) and Chiswick (1999) infers the requirement for specific systems (Heckman, 1979) to reliably assess causal instruments behind settler change. The effect of migration on the host work advertise has been demonstrated by Chiswick, Chiswick and Karras (1992) and Chiswick (1998). An enormous assortment of experimental writing, condensed by Kahanec and Zimmermann (2008), gives blended proof on the sign and determinants of these impacts on wages and business. 2 All the more as of late, the jobs of intermarriage (Meng and Gregory,

2005), citizenship (Bratsberg, Ragan and Nasir, 2002), informal communities (Munshi, 2003), and perspectives (Bauer, Lofstrom and Zimmermann, 2000; Kahanec and Tosun, 2009) concerning foreigner alteration have gotten significant consideration. The idea of ethnic personality has been reached out by Consistent and Zimmermann (2008), who expound on how connection to the nation of root and the host nation influence outsider alteration. In spite of the fact that estimating the impacts of movement is a nontrivial work, relocation without a doubt influences the prosperity of the entire society and all things considered, has become a significant and touchy approach issue. It is particularly the inquiries of the work advertise results of relocation, worker change in have social orders, and government assistance rivalry that have gotten significant arrangement consideration. Understanding the circumstances and end results of universal relocation streams requires a sound and inside and out examination. The requirement for such investigation is generally obvious in the investigation of causal connections, as these are difficult to build up experimentally and their deception bargains both scientific and strategy examinations. Truth be told, it might prompt off base approach proposals, which may prompt flighty outcomes or even impacts in opposition to those planned. Since such investigation is outlandish without top notch information, such information are crucial for approach investigators just as researchers.

Which information are accessible and utilized?

In spite of the general shortage of movement information, researchers and examiners have had the option to utilize some current overview or regulatory datasets just as little scope committed review information to consider relocation issues. While these datasets have encouraged significant research, missing factors, unnecessary anonymization, and imperfections in information assortment configuration regularly bargain researchers' endeavors to expand and extend our insight into relocation circumstances and end results. In this segment we center around some huge scope datasets gathered at the European level, as they, as opposed to little scope overviews, have an inborn potential to give the important transnational, longitudinal and orderly information assortment system. There are four broad datasets that spread in some measurement European movement directions: European People group Family unit Board (ECHP), EU Insights on Pay and Day to day environments (EU-SILC), EU Work Power Overview (EU-LFS), and the OECD/SOPEMI dataset. Each of these datasets contains data about demography, work power cooperation, business, joblessness, independent work, and instructive accomplishment of outsiders. Furthermore, the European Social Study (ESS) covers individuals' perspectives towards foreigners just as their democratic inclinations, in this way tending to relocation in a roundabout way. Table 1 portrays the character of these datasets, featuring a portion of their qualities and shortcomings. We can identify in any event three significant holes in the accessible data.3 Initially, these datasets give none or just an extremely restricted record of relocation directions. Transnational relocation directions may include straightforward or redundant moves between at least two nations with transitory spells of different lengths just as perpetual moves. It is practically difficult to track such directions – with every one of their spells, stops, and circularities – inside Europe, and among Europe and third nations. Specifically, no or little data is accessible on transients' understanding before their appearance to the nation of current home or their aims on further moves. Besides, the information ordinarily license deciding worker status dependent on a person's citizenship and nation of inception, ignoring the enormous gatherings of individuals with a settler foundation who are local residents, or those with double citizenships. At long last, anonymization regularly renders any important investigation inconceivable, for instance, when outsiders from altogether different sources (for example Zimbabwe and Japan) are assembled into one classification (for example non-EU).

Information get to issues and needs Deficient access to existing datasets is one of the most restricting components for scientific and strategy investigation. Because of prohibitive information get to arrangements, an absence of enthusiasm on the authorities mindful, misconstrued information insurance rules, or simply the absence of satisfactory information get to foundation, the utilization of datasets for scientific and approach objects is, when all is said in done, seriously constrained. Since movement is, by definition, a transnational and dynamic wonder (for example including single direction just as rehash, successive and round development between more nations), its legitimate examination requires a mix of data from more nations and across more periods.

Accordingly, limitations on information get to and an absence of coordination of access rules are especially hindering to the examination of movement issues. Beneath we show probably the most problems that are begging to be addressed that hinder accessibility of information for movement examination and decide the necessities concerning assortment of satisfactory information on relocation. One of the fundamental issues is that identifying and characterizing vagrants in the current datasets is anything but an insignificant issue. The movement foundation, remote root (outside conceived), citizenship, or ethnicity can be utilized to decide if somebody is an outsider. Tragically, just a subset of this data, if any, is accessible in existing datasets. No one but infrequently would one be able to identify first, second, and further ages of foreigners, residents and non-residents, and recognize settlers of different starting point and ethnicity. It is much more rare conceivable to get data that describes relocation directions. Maybe except for length of remain in the host nation, pre-relocation experience, track of all relocation moves, or movement directions of relatives (life partners) are not really accessible. While the absence of information portraying relocation directions of the individuals who make increasingly visit, perhaps roundabout, moves is a general issue, it is especially tricky on account of high-expertise transients, as these are the most liquid and versatile section of the vagrant populace.

Other important and frequently missing data incorporate language, religion, and connection to the host society and the nation of inception. A further related issue is that the impacts of out-relocation are difficult to catch, as we normally don't watch individuals who leave or their qualities (they don't deregister and are in a different nation when information are gathered). Truth be told, this lack makes issues for the investigation of the whole populace also, since it bargains the representativeness of datasets. For instance, as indicated by the

Week by week Report of the German Organization for Monetary Exploration (Wochenbericht des DIW) (2008, p. 382),. questions emerged in Germany with regards to whether the official enumeration measurements despite everything spoke to the real truth of the German populace. As the German national registration information has just been founded on registers since 1987 – which rely upon legitimate enlisting and deregistering of individuals – the individuals who leave the nation and don't deregister are incorrectly checked. A case of the size of the estimation blunder which can come about because of neglecting to follow out-relocation of the individuals who have not deregistered was uncovered in a tidy up of the information from the German Focal Register of Outsiders (Ausländerzentralregister) in 2004, which indicated that the official enumeration insights had exaggerated the quantity of outsiders in Germany by around 600,000. Another difficulty is that most datasets are illustrative of the all out populace and contain a predetermined number of perceptions. While this shouldn't be an issue in different settings, with regards to relocation it regularly suggests inadequate examples of the settler populace. Moreover, numerous datasets are cross-sectional and along these lines don't catch the dynamic idea of relocation. Specifically, the depiction picture that such datasets give can however catch the latest move and can't recognize some significant impacts, for example, those of host nation experience and migrant companion on outsider modification. At long last, information on relocation aims and reasons, and their relationship to genuine movement choices is basic for anticipating future movement streams just as for understanding vagrants' results in the host social orders. Exact assessments of the bearings and qualities of such streams are urgent for planning powerful and proficient movement arrangements, for example with regards to EU extension. The goals to remain, to be specific, regardless of whether vagrants see their circumstance as impermanent or they come to settle in the host nation for all time, bears significant ramifications for their work showcase conduct and subsequently the impacts they apply on the host economy.

Is migration positive or negative? Some contend that settlers flood across outskirts, take occupations, are a weight on citizens and undermine indigenous culture. Others state the inverse: that migration supports monetary development, meets aptitude deficiencies, and makes an increasingly unique society.

Proof obviously shows that settlers give significant monetary advantages. In any case, there are nearby and transient monetary and social expenses. Similarly, as with banters on exchange, where protectionist impulses will in general overpower the more extended term requirement for increasingly open social orders, the center job that workers play in monetary advancement is regularly overpowered by cautious apportions to keep outsiders. An answer should be found through strategies that permit the advantages to make up for the misfortunes.

Around the globe, there are an expected 230 million transients, making up about 3% of the worldwide populace. This offer has not changed much in the previous 100 years. However, as the total populace has quadrupled, so too has the quantity of vagrants. Also, since the mid 1900s, the quantity of nations has expanded from 50 to more than 200. More fringes mean more vagrants.

Of the worldwide yearly progression of around 15 million transients, generally fit into one of four classes: monetary (6 million), understudy (4 million), family (2 million), and exile/haven (3 million). There are around 20 million formally perceived outcasts around the world, with 86% of them facilitated by neighboring nations, up from 70% 10 years back.

In the US, over 33% of archived migrants are gifted. Comparative patterns exist in Europe. These rates mirror the necessities of those economies. Governments that are progressively open to movement help their nation's organizations, which become increasingly coordinated, versatile and beneficial in the war for ability. Governments thusly get more income and residents blossom with the dynamism that profoundly gifted vagrants bring.

However, it isn't just higher-gifted vagrants who are indispensable. In the USA and somewhere else, untalented outsiders are a basic piece of the development, farming and administrations division.

If workers assume such an imperative job, why is there so much concern?

Some accept that workers take occupations and decimate economies. Proof refutes this. In the US, migrants have been authors of organizations, for example, Google, Intel, PayPal, eBay, and Yippee! Truth be told, talented settlers represent over portion of Silicon Valley new businesses and over portion of licenses, despite the fact that they make up under 15% of the populace. There have been three-fold the number of outsider Nobel Laureates, National Institute of Science individuals, and Foundation Grant movie executives than the worker portion of the populace would anticipate. Research presumed that "settlers extend the economy's beneficial limit by invigorating speculation and advancing specialization, which produces proficiency gains and lifts pay per laborer".

Research on the net financial effect of movement shows that workers contribute significantly more in charges than the advantages and administrations they get consequently. expanding movement by an edge equivalent to 3% of the workforce in created nations would produce worldwide monetary increases of $356 billion. A few financial analysts foresee that if fringes were totally open and laborers were permitted to go where they satisfied, it would create gains as high as $39 trillion for the world economy more than multi year

Later on, it will turn out to be considerably progressively basic to guarantee a solid work supply enlarged by remote laborers. All around, the populace is maturing. There were just 14 million individuals beyond 80 1950 years old in 1950. There are well more than 100 million today and current projections show there will be about 400 million individuals more than 80 by 2050. With richness falling to underneath substitution levels in all areas aside from Africa, specialists are foreseeing quickly rising reliance proportions and a decrease in the OECD workforce from around 800 million to near 600 million by 2050. The issue is especially intense in North America, Europe and Japan.

There are, be that as it may, authentic worries about huge scope movement. The chance of social separation is genuine. Much the same as globalization – a solid power for good on the planet – the constructive perspectives are diffuse and regularly elusive, while the contrary angles nibble hard for a little gathering of individuals.

Truly, those negative perspectives must be overseen. In any case, that administration must accompany the acknowledgment that relocation has consistently been one of the most significant drivers of human advancement and dynamism. Movement is acceptable. What's more, in the time of globalization, hindrances to relocation represent a danger to monetary development and supportability. Free relocation, as thoroughly organized commerce, stays an idealistic possibility, despite the fact that inside locales, (for example, Europe) this has demonstrated serviceable.

In the twenty first century, global relocation contacts the lives of more individuals than any time in recent memory. Within excess of 160 million individuals assessed to be living outside their nation of birth, practically no nation is immaculate by worldwide movement or is resistant to its belongings. With neediness, political constraint, human rights misuses, and struggle driving into an ever increasing number of individuals out of their nations of origin while financial chances, political opportunity, physical wellbeing, and security pull both exceptionally gifted and incompetent laborers into new terrains, it is accepted that the pace of universal movement is probably not going to slow in future.

Recorded mankind's history is dabbed with 'periods of movement'. From the Greek settlements and roman military victories through the Byzantine and hassock domains, and from the European colonisations to the extraordinary relocations of the nineteenth and mid twentieth hundred of years, movement has been noteworthy to human advancements as scarcely any other huge social wonders have (Spencer, Sarah).

Not very many nations stayed immaculate by movement. Countries as fluctuated as Haiti, India and the previous Yugoslavia feed universal streams. The US gets by a long shot the most universal transients, however vagrants additionally fill Germany, France, Canada, Saudi Arabia, and Iran. A few nations, similar to Mexico, send displaced people to different nations, yet additionally get foreigners both those wanting to settle and the individuals who are on their way somewhere else.

So relocation of individuals to nations has happened all through history and it is in no way, shape or form another marvel. What's going on is the changing idea of movement in this time of globalization. In this globalize world, where everything is by all accounts worldwide, movement is additionally changing its tendency and structures which it takes.

The popular expression globalization, similar to a tsunami, has conveyed with it numerous social and monetary elements that are currently characterized as far as globalizing inclinations. Universal relocation is no special case to this. In any case, what precisely globalization has done to movement is a real and significant inquiry. For some, universal movement has gotten worldwide, to the extent that globalization implies more noteworthy course of products, individuals and capital and furthermore more noteworthy speed in world governmental issues. Globalization has changed the idea of worldwide relocation quantitatively, yet in addition subjectively. Globalization has activated more prominent portability, and there are subjective changes in relocation elements presented by the assorted variety of districts and individuals currently associated with the procedure of movement.

Elements WHICH LEAD TO Movement

Supply side components: – War and enormous scope catastrophes, whether characteristic or man made, are evident movement triggers as individuals escape for their lives. Past them, the underlying foundations of worldwide movement can be found in the mission to shield oneself and one's family from continued physical peril and to get away from emotional decreases in financial open doors that have gotten constant. The last reason for relocation is subjectively different from the quest for financial improvement, which is a steady component of movement (Spencer, Sarah).

As indicated by Spencer, two components within these two wide causes are probably going to stay significant drivers in the following two decades. The first is political, social and social bigotry; at the extraordinary, net, bunch based infringement of human rights. The second is the orderly disappointment of governments to change issues of total weakness: the different types of monetary prohibition and ethno-racial, strict or phonetic segregation that methodicallly hindrance certain portions of a populace. Both of these relocation drivers are constantly present, to a more noteworthy or lesser degree.

She likewise discusses three extra causes which require separate notice since they have as of late picked up in both harmfulness and significance. The first is inside and out ethno racial and additionally strict clash in which constraining the focused on gathering to desert the challenged region isn't just a result of the contention however a significant approach objective. The second includes the crumbling of biological systems to the point of making life unreasonable prime occurrences are jeopardized water security and broad corruption in water quality, the defilement of essential groceries and the results of desertification. The third concerns the departure from different types of normal and man made catastrophes.

Request side elements: – There are different elements influencing relocation like segment factors, monetary elements and so on. Due to low paces of local populace growth over the progressed modern world, movement is as of now a huge segment power. Somewhere in the range of 1985 and 1990, universal transients represented around one fourth of the built up total populace growth. That figure developed to around 45 percent during the period 1990-1995: a component of expanded migration and determinedly low ripeness (Spencer, Sarah).

Overall richness rates are falling, although creating nations keep on observing quick populace growth. In most industrialized nations, ripeness levels are well underneath substitution rates. In Europe, the assert age number of kids conceived per lady is 1.4; Italy's fruitfulness rate is 1.2. Nations with declining ripeness face the probability of a fall in complete populace, driving a few demographers to see an approaching populace implosion. Such countries can likewise anticipate a maturing populace, with less working-age individuals for each more established individual. Although migration won't take care of the issue, it will assist ease with working deficiencies and change to some degree the maturing of the general public (Martin, F. Susan).

Segment drifts likewise help clarify displacement pressures in Africa, Latin America, and a few pieces of Asia, where ripeness rates are high. Quickly developing social orders regularly can't produce enough occupations to stay up with new passages into the work power. Growth may likewise cause ecological debasement, especially when land use strategies don't ensure delicate biological systems. Catastrophic events likewise unleash ruin on thickly populated zones in poor nations (Martin, F. Susan).

Monetary factors likewise impact the relocation designs. Most theorists consent to these components answerable for movement. Susan clarifies that Financial patterns impact movement designs from numerous points of view. Worldwide partnerships, for instance, press administer to ease developments of administrators, chiefs, and other key faculty starting with one nation then onto the next. At the point when work deficiencies show up, whether in data innovation or regular horticulture, organizations additionally try to import remote laborers to fill employments.

As per Susan, The growth in worldwide exchange and venture likewise influences source nations. Financial improvement has for quite some time been viewed as the best long haul answer for migration pressures emerging from the absence of monetary open doors in creating nations. Uniformly, in any case, specialists alert that resettlement pressures are probably going to remain and, perhaps, increment before the drawn out advantages gather. Wayne

Cornelius and Philip Martin hypothesize that as building up nations' wages start to rise and chances to venture out from home increment, displacement first increments and decreases just later as pay differentials among resettlement and movement nations fall. Italy and Korea, in moving from displacement to migration nations, offer confidence to that theory.

Geopolitical changes since the Virus War period offer both chances and difficulties for overseeing worldwide relocation, especially displaced person developments. During the Virus War, the US and other Western nations considered exile to be as an instrument of international strategy. The Virus War made it everything except difficult to address the foundations of displaced person developments, which frequently came about because of surrogate clashes in Southeast Asia, Focal America, Afghanistan, and the Horn of Africa. Hardly any evacuees had the option or ready to come back to lands despite everything commanded by strife or Socialism. With the finish of the Virus War, new chances to return rose as decades-old clashes reached a conclusion. Democratization and expanded regard for human rights grabbed hold in numerous nations, as saw in the once in the past Socialist nations of East Europe, making repatriation a reality for many exiles who had been uprooted for a considerable length of time (Martin, F. Susan).

Sociological clarifications of relocation center around the significance of social and social capital. Social capital alludes to information on other social orders and the open doors they offer, just as data about how to really approach moving and looking for work somewhere else. Obviously, globalization helps make this social capital accessible by radiating pictures of Western lifestyles into the most remote towns. Improved proficiency and fundamental instruction likewise add to the capacity to move. Social capital alludes to the associations expected to relocate securely and cost-viably. It is notable that most vagrants follow 'beaten paths' and go where their countrymen have just settled a bridgehead, making it simpler to look for some kind of employment and lodgings, and manage bureaucratic deterrents. More seasoned relocation researchers talked about 'chain movement,' while lately much accentuation has been put on 'relocation systems' and the way these create as connections between networks at home and in goal zones. These systems are greatly encouraged by the improved interchanges and transport advances of globalization, and are therefore picking up in strength and striking nature. Systems are a further factor that supports and change relocation when the first reason for a development is expelled. For example, when the German government halted work movement from Turkey in 1973, streams proceeded and developed looking like family get-together, refuge searchers and illicit vagrants which all pre-owned travel paths and network foundations set up in the past period (Martin, 1991).

Along these lines, the greater part of the theorists and researchers have consented to some basic variables prompting relocation. The most evident and well known explanation given – the draw from higher wages in labor accepting nations. So the push factors for this situation are significant levels of joblessness and destitution in source nations which push the choices of locals to move from their nation of birthplace to one having work openings with higher wages.

Additionally, now and again, systems of companions and

family members, previously working in goal nations fill in as wellsprings of data and grapple networks for newcomers. So tricked by companions and family members and informal organization relocation can occur.

Additionally, it isn't just these variables which cause work relocation, however it is in light of a legitimate concern for nations to advance movement. Work sending nations advance relocation since they have a few intentions. First is the monstrous local joblessness and second is acquiring of remote trade. Work sending nations advance relocation, as this gives some help as far as work as these nations particularly the creating nations which have issues of high joblessness and destitution. Desires of instructed laborers for higher wages likewise lead them to other nations. Now and then, the understudies travel to another country for study purposes and settle there, as work openings and higher wages pulls in them.

- Furthermore, movement moreover fills in as wellspring of remote salary. Duty of worker settlements to remote exchange benefit is the significant favorable position that is gotten by work sending countries. This could be one inspiration driving why countries may bolster migration and support it.

- In this way, movement is unquestionably not another wonder thus the factors are in like manner not new. What's happening is the nature and structures which movement is taking in the present overall world.

- Globalization is a significant primary purpose of overall work movement. In articulations of Stalker: –

- "In a vast expanse of champs and disappointments, the

wastes of time don't simply evaporate; they search for somewhere else to go". (Stalker, 2000)

- It bodes well that globalization with its related movement systems achieved an immense augmentation in adaptability of work across borders as by virtue of capital and development. Houses (1999) keeps up that globalization will when all is said in done disintegrate the force and independence of the nation state and that overall movement is an essential bit of globalization. Globalization has made development much more straightforward through better correspondences, dissipating of information through wide interchanges and improved vehicle, among others. It is the extending trade and theory streams in various regions, which empowered interest and care in movement.

- "The continuous expansion of the overall correspondences arrange – telephone affiliations, satellite dishes and video rental stores – has recently significantly influenced the perception of the world's less prosperous social requests. Horizons have been extended, wants raised and social differences diminished. The photos gave by such media may be, all things considered, sham. Nevertheless, they pass on an extraordinary message about the focal points experienced by people living in the made states". (UNHCR, 1995)

- Globalization powers have strengthened the improvement of gifted workers who move with FDI streams and overall hypotheses. Capable administrators, extraordinarily gifted individuals and experts are welcomed by various countries to pull in remote endeavor.

- Globalization has similarly extended monetary irregularities between countries. Stalker (2000) fights that movements of product and capital among rich and poor countries won't be adequately colossal to balance the prerequisites for work in increasingly terrible countries. For instance, "the social interference realized by money related reconstructing is most likely going to shake more people liberated from their systems and urge them to look abroad for work." (Stalker, 2000).

- On the "obfuscated side of globalization", some have fought that globalization adds to higher managing and conveying of individuals across borders with the proliferation of transnationals bad behavior syndicates. (Linard, 1998).

- However, paying little mind to specific differences, each and every significant theorist by separating the examples lead to a near end, that migration is extending in the overall universe of today and it is presumably going to create in not all that removed future.

- Two essential models of migration and solidification managed insightful and procedure approaches in the late twentieth century: first, the explorer model, according to which untouchables a little bit at a time composed into financial and social relations, re-consolidated or molded families and at long last got consumed into the host society (once in a while in excess of a couple of ages); second, the fleeting development model, as showed by which transient workers stayed in the host country for a confined period, and kept up their union with their country of root. Globalization, portrayed as a proliferation of cross-periphery streams and transnationals frameworks, has changed the setting for movement. New advances of correspondence and transport grant visit and multi-directional movements of people, thoughts and social pictures. The breaking down of nation state force and self-rule cripples systems of edge control and transient assimilation. The result is the difference in the material and social practices related with development and system course of action, and the clouding of cutoff points between different classes of homeless people (Houses, Stephen, 2002).

- The principal work development plays in the front line society can be seen as a steady, yet its character and structures changes with respect to fiscal and social shifts and progression in advancement and culture. Thusly, the specific characteristics of migration changed in the current conditions of globalization. Globalization isn't just a fiscal marvel: stream of capital, product and adventures can not occur without equivalent movements of thoughts, social things and people. These streams tend continuously to be sifted through transnationals frameworks of the most changed sorts, going from intergovernmental affiliations and transnationals ventures through to widespread NGOs and overall criminal syndicates (Held et al., 1999).

HOW Types OF Movement Evolving?

Strongholds identifies three fundamental ways to deal with joining of outsiders into society: osmosis, differential prohibition and multiculturalism. In more established understandings of significant distance relocation, newcomers were relied upon to move for all time and cut off connections with their place of inception, so they and their relatives in the end turned out to be completely acclimatized into the accepting society. As a method of fuse, absorption implies urging foreigners to become familiar with the national language and to completely embrace the social and social acts of the accepting network. This includes an exchange of devotion from the spot of birth to the new nation and the reception of another national personality.

In any case, not the sum total of what settlers have been viewed as assimilable. Indeed, even the US has had impermanent movement plans, similar to the Bracero Program for Mexican farmworkers. In addition, not all movement nations have attempted to absorb outsiders. Indeed, even before the mechanical upsets in Europe, practices of enlisting transitory vagrant specialists were normal (Moch, 1992, 1995). In the late nineteenth century, such plans got regulated in France, Germany and Switzerland with a high level of control by the state and businesses' associations. In post-1945 Europe, 'guestworker' or impermanent work enrollment frameworks assumed a significant job in labor advertise arrangements. 'Guestworkers' were intended to originate from generally proximate nations of root – particularly the European fringe – and reserved no privilege to family gathering or perpetual remain. All the more as of late, comparable methodologies have been utilized in Inlet oil nations and Asian NICs. This method of joining is alluded to as differential prohibition since it implies that transients are coordinated briefly into certain cultural sub-frameworks, for example, the work market and restricted government assistance qualifications, however avoided from others, for example, political interest and national culture (Mansions, 2002).

In any case, both digestion and differential prohibition share a significant regular rule: that migration ought not achieve significant changes in the getting society. Such convictions in the controllability of ethnic difference could be supported previously, yet started to be addressed from the 1970s in Western migration nations. In the 'visitor laborer' nations, impermanent vagrants were transforming into pioneers. Just states got themselves unequipped for expelling enormous quantities of undesirable specialists. Nor could workers be totally denied social rights, since this would prompt genuine clashes and divisions. The outcome was family get-together, network arrangement and development of new ethnic minorities. In traditional movement nations, the desire for long haul social digestion demonstrated fanciful, with ethnic networks keeping up their dialects and societies into the second and third ages. Outsiders started to set up social affiliations, spots of love and ethnic organizations – patterns which soon additionally got significant throughout Western Europe (Strongholds, 2000).

The outcome was the presentation of legitimate strategies of multiculturalism, at first in Canada (1971) and Australia (1973). In the US, multi-culturalism has a to some degree different importance, connected to understandings of the job of minorities in culture and history (Gitlin, 1995; Steinberg, 1995). Here pluralism was utilized to allude to acknowledgment of social and strict decent variety for migrants – for the most part in the private circle rather than as government approach. Rather comparative approaches with shifting marks, (for example, minorities' strategy in the Netherlands) before long followed in European movement nations. Now and again they were presented uniquely in specific parts, for example, government assistance or instruction, or at the city or common rather than the national level (Held, 1999).

There is boundless acknowledgment that social and social changes realized by movement are unavoidable truths that apply to everyone, which must be perceived in different territories. This can be viewed as one of the significant effects of movement: in only a couple of ages, old myths of national uniqueness and homogeneity have been subverted.

Globalization prompts significant changes in the character of universal movement. The setting for transient fuse has just changed drastically and will keep on evolving. The ascent of multiculturalism itself is one indication of this. Yet, this isn't all; new types of personalities and effects go past multiculturalism. At the beginning of the twenty-first century, globalization is subverting all the methods of controlling difference prefaced on territoriality. Expanding versatility; growth of impermanent, recurrent and repeating relocations; modest and simple travel; consistent correspondence through new data innovations: all inquiry the possibility of the individual who has a place with only one country state or at most moves from one state to only one other (whether briefly or forever). These progressions have prompted banters on the significance of transnationalism and transnationals networks as new methods of vagrant having a place. Transnationals people group are bunches whose character isn't principally founded on connection to a specific domain. They therefore present an incredible test to conventional thoughts of country state having a place ((Bauman, 1998).

transnational people group give off an impression of being proliferating quickly at present. This pattern can maybe best be comprehended as a feature of procedures of worldwide joining and time-space pressure. This is halfway a mechanical issue: improved vehicle and open continuous electronic correspondence is the material premise of globalization. Be that as it may, over all it is a social and social issue: globalization is firmly connected to changes in social structures and connections, and to shifts in social qualities worried about spot, portability and having a place. This is probably going to have significant results, which we are just barely starting to comprehend (Bauman, 1998; Held et al, 1999). It is conceivable that transnational affiliations and cognizance will turn into the prevalent type of vagrant having a place later on. This would have extensive results.

Worldwide movement has constantly supported in social trades and - notwithstanding the difficulties raised when people, gatherings and networks of different societies, ethnic gatherings and religions live respectively it is sensible to expect that it will keep on producing multicultural spaces and spread thoughts and qualities. Globalization includes contradicting developments, be that as it may: desires for versatility become across the board, yet the limitations on development become more tightly constantly. The new innovations in the fields of correspondences and transport encourage universal portability, and besides, thanks to better tutoring, together with more data on the circumstance in other nations - with messages on ways of life and codes of qualities which uplift the view of the alleged points of interest of movement there are currently a lot more people keen on relocating.

In the last examination, the option to move is a possibility for every one of those with at least human capital who can't appear their desires to social versatility in their nations of cause, whose limitations on the activity of financial and social rights end up by sabotaging the option to remain. Thus, global developments of people and families - looking for something that their own nations just offer them emblematically depend on progressively educated choices, joined by the discernment that such moves include diminishing dangers and expenses. This is the present demeanor to relocation, the intentions where are currently generally free of absolutely monetary contemplations.

One of the social manifestations of globalization is the change from regionally based national personalities to others which are maybe less far reaching yet are of a trans-regional nature. Relocation has prompted the rise of new entertainers who, composed in networks and connected together through systems, keep up close connections with their territories of starting point (to which they send settlements and data) and speak to aggregate referents of character in the regions of goal (Portes, 1997a). These transnational networks are an away from of the intelligent job of worldwide relocation and globalization within the setting of the blast of character denoting the discontinuity of social orders today (Castells, 1999, vol. II).

Interpersonal organizations and networks structure some portion of an agreed methodology of transients with regards to their social highlights, the outflow of their requests for citizenship, and assurance both from prohibitive mentalities to migration and practices of social dismissal (as exemplified in the working states of numerous vagrants and hostile to movement emotions). To an enormous degree, they go about as criticism factors advancing movement streams and further the diversification of human versatility.

The transnational networks profit by the customary relationship of transients, however they are more unpredictable than these: they advance social occasions - moves, suppers, merriments and common items and they legitimize the decent variety of the beneficiary social orders. They are topographically expanded social units, with close relations and steady connections, and even support transnational miniaturized scale enterprising activities (Portes, 1997a and 1997b). They frequently work with strains, clashes and inconsistencies that reproduce the setting of basic disparity of their networks of cause, and thereby fill in as a framework for the social proliferation of their individuals in their goal nations (Canales and Zlolniski, 2000).8 The heterogeneity of their individuals, the capability of some of them for obstruction and resistance, their different types of association, their universal connections and their perplexing relations with the market and the State make these transnational networks a required component of reference of unquestionable significance for the plan of measures to manage the topic of relocation. Their intelligent connection with globalization is especially obvious on account of Latin

WORLD ECONOMY CHANGES

The worldwide financial scene has experienced significant changes since the finish of the Virus War. After the worldwide money related emergency, the world economy entered "another typical," and there are mounting moves that should be overseen. Tragically, the worldwide administration framework has not stayed up with the scale and unpredictability of these difficulties.

The world economy's post-war design was developed by the U.S. to an enormous degree, with the intention to recreate a liberal universal financial framework. The Universal Money Reserve (IMF), the World Bank, and the General Concession to Tariffs and Trade (GATT) established the framework for the after-war worldwide monetary request, and global exchange and capital streams step by step began to continue. To solidify its matchless quality in the shadow of the Cold War, the U.S. upheld the financial advancement of its partners through a guide, for example, the Marshall Plan focused on Western Europe and colossal subsidizing coordinated to Japan during the Korean War. In any event, during the 1970s, U.S. authority started to melt away, as a large group of nations emerging from the post-war National Freedom Development ran to the Assembled Countries, squeezing out for a purported New Global Monetary Request that would be more in favor of Third World nations. Furthermore, the 1973 breakdown of the Bretton Woods framework suggested that the U.S. needed to rely more on macroeconomic strategy coordination instruments with other created nations to preserve the universal money related request.

The ejection of the 1997–1998 Asian money related emergency started broad doubt of the way of administration received by the IMF and the "Washington Agreement" behind it. It quickened a rising consciousness of local collaboration across Asia. The episode of the 2007 subprime contract emergency in the US, just as the 2010 sovereign obligation emergency in Europe, changed the since quite a while ago settled conviction that created economies are inoculated from money related emergencies. As the worldwide financial framework has gotten progressively unequipped for managing the recognition, anticipation, and treatment of emergencies brought about by the flood of globalization, provincial or cross-local monetary administration stages are playing an always significant job. This advancement can be seen in the multilateralization of the Chiang Mai Activity, the strengthening of the BRICS, and the growth of uber territorial unhindered commerce understanding exchanges like the Provincial Thorough Monetary Organization (RCEP), Trans-Pacific Association (TPP), and Trans-Atlantic Exchange and Venture Organization (TTIP).

Despite various difficulties, the essential design of the world economy remains, to a great extent, unaltered. Also, the change of the present universal financial framework should concentrate on three primary issues.

To begin with, the superpower status of the US

is being tested by its similar reduction of strength.

Total U.S. national production (Gross domestic product)

was at number

one spot until 2003 when the European Union (EU) surpassed it.

According to observations discharged by the World Bank, U.S. gross domestic product added up to 30.6 percent of the world's aggregate in

2000, although by 2015 the figure had subsequently fallen to 24.3 percent.1 the U.S. portion of universal exchange and speculation has declined considerably. Notwithstanding the fiscal authority that the U.S. dollar has kept up for quite a long time, the production of the euro has subverted its outright strength, which, together with the stewing obligation issue tormenting the US, will steadily shake its status as a protected "cash asylum."

Furthermore, as the timid economy and growing unemployment have become its primary concerns, the US is not. At this stage, prepared to push global monetary growth and is shifting its concentration toward transplanting the residential emergency abroad trying to sustain its intensity in the global economy. In the domain of security and discretion, flippant conduct by the United States and part of its inadequate financial and conciliatory approaches have often damaged the global market and the nation's authority.

Second, the ascent of developing forces was relied upon to reorder the worldwide economy's engineering. Since the start of the twenty-first century, creating nations have kept up quick monetary growth, and their assembled strength is moving toward that of the Gathering of Seven industrialized nations (G7). As indicated by IMF gauges, in 2001, G7 countries represented almost 43.435 percent of the world's complete Gross domestic product as far as buying power equality, yet in 2015 their offer declined to 31.5 percent. During a similar period, the monetary offer held by BRICS nations has expanded from 19.3 percent to more than 30.8 percent of the world's total.2 Creation of nations has been another significant impetus in the world economy in the last few years. In addition, they have started to engage in the world's top-level administration plan and therefore expect an undeniably significant job in certain significant establishments worldwide. This circumstance is reflected most importantly in the ascent of the Gathering of Twenty (G20), which includes major created and creating economies and established. It is the most critical stage of monetary collaboration in the world. Tragically, creating nations have still not picked up the status or voice proportionate to their strength and the force of their financial growth in the global monetary framework. One explanation is that rising forces are confronting the quandary of "twofold personality" as enormous yet creating nations. All things considered, the redistribution of interests, commitments, and force involved by the ascent of creating nations would influence the universal request explosively. The inquiry with regards to whether or not to acknowledge and deal with the ascent of creating nations is critical in determining if the present worldwide framework is versatile and stable.

Third, the new issues that have posed a potential threat since the emission of the worldwide budgetary emergency raised doubt about the liberal universal monetary framework. As the rule of facilitated commerce denoted the after war worldwide monetary request, the previous decades have seen enormous scope financial globalization, and nations embraced change measures and an approach of opening-up, dealt with universal undertakings agreeably, and composed powerful strategies. Nonetheless, in the aftermath of the worldwide budgetary emergency, globalization has been ebbing for it uncovered irregular monetary characteristics, imbalances, and other social clashes that had been covered by fast global growth. More terrifyingly, signs of the worldwide monetary emergency started spilling from the monetary and money related to the social and political part, causing strife in certain areas and nations. Having witnessed worldwide money-related misfortunes, far-reaching chaos, and internal conflicts, individuals around the world have been increasingly worried about the inefficiency and utilization of worldwide wealth. The quest for value and equity has become an ongoing and progressively well-known pattern.

As U.S. power in the world economy continues to decline as China becomes the world's largest economy by 2024, creating nations expands, and new issues develop, the worldwide monetary request enters an apparently divided stage. Others may highlight the downside of China's ascension and are concerned that China plans to challenge the predominant status of the U.S. in the worldwide financial request. It's not really the truth. Indeed, the Asian Foundation Speculation Bank (AIIB) and Belt and Street Activity are likely to reshape the financial geology in the affected locations and thus have an impact on the worldwide monetary scene. However, it doesn't really imply that China wants to replace U.S. administration in the global economy. Rather, China means to submit to current worldwide guidelines and foundations while accepting merited obligations equivalent to its universal status. Not only because rising forces, including China, have all gained a lot from the after war worldwide financial request and a quiet universal condition. But more importantly, the universal network needs a specific way of dealing with growth and a serious point of view with resistance to improving other nations as the fundamental belief, that implies supreme authority in the worldwide monetary request must turn into a thing of the past.

All the developments in the global financial request involve the redistribution of universal responsibility as a global force. Rising powers, including China, should endorse a stance that endures worldwide advancement. Developing such a basic belief would help rising forces attempt worldwide duties proportionate to their present national strength and chronicled imperialism, preventing them from trusted with duties and obligations beyond their capacity. Simultaneously, such an attitude towards advancing other nations would likewise request that created nations embrace their obligations, perform their duties, and provide more consideration to the sensible requests of less created nations. This will undoubtedly have a worldwide impact and will convert into an increasingly comprehensive worldwide financial request sooner rather than later.

Exchange strains among China and the U.S. re-raised in August, after the declaration by the U.S. that it will force tariffs on a further $300 billion of Chinese imports. In counter, China presented extra tariffs on $75 billion of imports from the U.S. These advancements activated sharp developments in worldwide value advertisements, a decrease in worldwide oil costs, and higher capital outpourings from the rising economies. As the exchange questions threaten to turn out to be significantly increasingly inescapable, the worldwide growth standpoint has obscured.

Given uncertain exchange dealings, there is a developing danger that exchange pressures will escalate further in the future. If the U.S. extends prohibitive exchange measures, for instance, by imposing tariffs on vehicle imports, affected nations will probably respond with retaliatory measures. Such a winding of further tariffs and reprisals would spread beyond the included gatherings, affecting both immediate and backhanded channels in the creating economies.

Higher tariffs and delayed powerless opinions could significantly hose residential interest growth in the significant economies, to be specific China, United States, and Europe. This will legitimately influence economies with a high last interest introduction to these huge markets. Figure 2 shows that China is the principle wellspring of definite interest for some East Asian exporters today, including Malaysia, the Republic of Korea, and Thailand. For these economies, this mirrors a stamped change in the exchange structure contrasted with ten years prior, when a bigger portion of fares was cooked towards request in the US and Europe. Interestingly, nations, for example, Costa Rica and Mexico, stay substantially more helpless against a growth stoppage in the US. At the same time, the Russian Alliance and Turkey are progressively touchy to changes in the European interest. Likewise, more slow growth in China and the US would burden worldwide interest for products, unfavorably affecting item subordinate nations, remembering for Africa and Latin America.

An intensifying of exchange strains will likewise indirectly affect third nations through disturbances to worldwide worth chains (GVCs). Nations that are profoundly incorporated into GVCs would be the most influenced by a diminishing sought after for halfway contributions, as the inconvenience of tariffs harms gathering nations, but also providers along creation chains. Remarkably, the exchange debates have amplified patterned headwinds in the hardware and vehicle segments, both of which have broad cross-country creation systems. In the main portion of 2019, world semiconductor billings declined by almost 15 percent in the main part of 2019 compared to a similar period a year ago. In the interim, worldwide car deals have contracted in the initial seven months of the year, as talked about later.

Furthermore, an intensification of the exchange struggle would fuel more prominent vulnerability in the worldwide condition, prompting an improved probability of firms delaying or dropping venture plans. Combined with relaxing worldwide interest and nation specific issues, ongoing information shows that growth in investment has eased back pointedly in many creating economies, including Mexico, the Republic of Korea, South Africa, and Singapore.

Besides, while exchange debates among China and the US could create open doors for a few nations, the overall impacts on the worldwide economy are negative. Present uncertain exchange strains will not solely draw out the shortcomings in worldwide exchange and request. Yet, they are fortunate to set off a broader range of protectionist quantifications by other nations, wrecking global financial action. Critically, the drawn-out exchange strife may inflict reliable harm on the possibilities of worldwide development. A stoppage in speculation would bring about more vulnerable job creation while obliging efficiency growth. In many creating nations, disturbances to GVCs could likewise extensively sabotage growth, given the significant job that GVC-related exchange has played in raising salary per capita and efficiency. The loss of salary may have an impact on social spending, though, for families, the expansion in costs of merchandise due to tariffs brings down buying force and purchaser government assistance, especially if residential and imported products are not effectively replaceable.

Amid compelled macroeconomic strategy space, an acceleration of exchange protectionism, the world economy represents a significant hazard to worldwide growth and the acknowledgment of the 2030 Plan. The debut SDG Summit, which will be held in the not so distant future, presents an important open door for world pioneers to take part in profitable exchange and talk about methodologies to address the current worldwide financial difficulties, including a strengthening of the principles-based multilateral exchanging framework.

Created economies

North America and Europe: Car creation contracts in the midst of lull in exchange

Following a 3.4 percent compression in 2018, the creation of cars in the US declined by a further 2 percent in the initial seven months of 2019. In the European Association, assembling of engine vehicles declined by more than 10 percent in the principal half of 2019. This feeble presentation of the car area frames some portion of a wide worldwide pattern. In 2018, the world creation of traveler vehicles declined by 0.9 percent, denoting the main worldwide constriction in this area since the worldwide money related emergency in 2008-09. Accessible information indicated a much greater restriction in 2019. The car business is one of the world's biggest monetary areas and is work and capital escalated. Its elements have an important impact on global development, business, and event turnaround.

In China, where vehicle deals between January and July 2019 were 11.4 percent lower compared to a year ago, powerless worldwide creation is generally credited to falling demand. Additionally, traveler vehicle enrollments have declined significantly in Australia, Canada, India, the US, and Europe. Germany is the world's largest car exporter, and Europe is especially vulnerable to a worldwide decline in vehicle interest.

Worldwide exchange strains have significantly upset creation in the car division, both through the immediate effect of higher tariffs and the circuitous effect of arrangement vulnerability. As featured before, the car area is profoundly implanted in worldwide and provincial worth chains, with complex and geologically scattered creation organizes, and is therefore exceptionally touchy to disturbances in exchange. The inconvenience of steel tariffs in the US in Walk 2018 has been felt intensely by the car systems associated with North America, while an all-encompassing time of vulnerability during the exchanges encompassing the US-Canada-Mexico Understanding additionally upset North American car creation systems. In April 2018, China and the US raised tariffs on reciprocal imports of numerous vehicles and vehicle parts, although China hence suspended certain tariffs in light of disturbances to the area. The US Government has delayed until November 2019 a choice on threatened tariffs of up to 25 percent on all imports of vehicles and vehicle parts, drawing out the arrangement vulnerability confronting the area.

Notwithstanding exchange tariffs, the worldwide car area is experiencing progress identified with ecological measures. For instance, more tightly outflows principles in Europe have prompted some brief interruption of creation systems, while the New Vitality Vehicle motivating forces in China have affected interest for conventional inward burning motor vehicles. Simultaneously, vehicle sharing and ride sharing plans are getting progressively well known, discouraging interest for proprietorship. These weights can be required to keep on affecting vehicle request designs going ahead.

Created Asia: Japanese fares declined over the primary portion of 2019

Over the first half of 2019, Japan's export volumes declined by 5.6 percent compared to the same period last year. Import volumes also fell, but to a smaller extent, by 1 percent. Given the rapid decline in exports, Japan's trade balance remains in deficit. The recent export decline indicates some shift in trade patterns. Exports to other Asian countries, including China and the Republic of Korea, have contracted steel, semiconductor parts, and semiconductor equipment exports with a rapid contraction. In comparison, exports to the United States of automobiles and semiconductor-making equipment have increased. Although Japan's overall imports of energy and metal products were contracting, its imports of these products from the United States expanded rapidly.

Economies on the move

CIS: China is a significant fare goal for the district

Financial and political understandings closed by the nations in the District of Autonomous States (CIS) have prompted a specific fracture of provincial exchange designs. From one viewpoint, the Eurasian Financial Association (EAEU) of Armenia, Belarus, Kazakhstan, Kyrgyzstan, and the Russian Alliance, built up in 2015, enlisted a consistent increment in its inward exchange 2017–2018. Then again, Georgia (not an individual from the CIS), Republic of Moldova, and Ukraine in 2014 consented to Affiliation Arrangements with the EU, containing Profound and Complete Unhindered commerce Understandings. Simultaneously, the EU turned into a significant fare goal for those nations, engrossing 65.7 percent of fares of the Republic of Moldova in 2017 and 42.7 percent of Ukrainian fares in 2018. The EAEU has additionally finished up different understandings, including an organized commerce concurrence with Viet Nam; In contrast, Georgia has arrived at a facilitated commerce concurrence with China, which went into power in 2018. Common exchange limitations between the Russian League and the vast majority of the OECD nations, embraced after the Crimea strife, just as exchange limitations between the Russian Organization and Ukraine, are obliging the area's exchange development potential.

The immediate effect of the progressing exchange debates on the locale is probably going to be constrained, given the moderately low level of cooperation in worldwide creation chains. Be that as it may, more fragile vitality costs and easing back worldwide interest, particularly from China, could significantly influence the locale's vitality exporters. For Kazakhstan and the Russian Organization, China is a significant fare showcase. Until the ongoing choice by the Russian Gazprom to buy gaseous petrol from Focal Asia, China was likewise the main shipper of Turkmenistan's petroleum gas. In July, the Russian Organization agreed with China to significantly build soybean and wheat fares to make up for diminished imports from the US, and there are additionally plans to expand pork fares to China.

Creating economies

Africa: High weakness to exchange strains in the midst of developing intra-local exchange

The US-China exchange strains have added to easing back interest in Africa's key exchanging accomplices, including China and the euro territory. This has led to lower product costs and more fragile interest for Africa's ware trades, just as some choppiness in money markets. In the main seven day stretch of August, amid a sharp acceleration in the exchange strife and expanded hazard avoidance by speculators, developing business sector monetary standards has been comprehensively softened. South Africa's rand, specifically, slipped to seven-week lows against the dollar.

African nations could be seriously influenced by a further heightening of the exchange struggle between China and the US. China is Africa's single biggest exchanging accomplice, while the US places fifth. Examination by the IMF demonstrates that intensified exchange pressures and expanded exchange approach vulnerability the US, more slow development in China, lower ware costs, and more tightly monetary conditions can bring down development in sub-Saharan Africa by 2 rate focuses this year, and 1½ rate focuses one year from now. The economies most influenced would beware, exporters, nations with significant linkages with China and worldwide markets, and those with enormous renegotiating needs.

Notwithstanding, against the background of expanded exchange boundaries remotely, the mainland has been sorting out the world's biggest unhindered commerce zone inside. In July, the pioneers of Benin and Nigeria marked the understanding for the African Mainland Facilitated commerce Region at a unique African Association meeting in Niger's capital, Niamey. The agreement has now been marked by 54 of 55 part conditions of the African Association.

East Asia: Easing back development prompts approach facilitating measures

The extended exchange struggle among China and the US is obviously influencing East Asia's fare development. In the second quarter of 2019, trades contracted across most economies in the area, with Indonesia, the Republic of Korea, and Singapore encountering the biggest decreases. Driving markers, for example, new fare requests and business suppositions, have additionally kept on crumbling, pointing towards proceeded with outer area shortcoming in the coming months. Another increase in exchange strains represents a significant drawback hazard to East Asia's development, especially given its capability to seriously upset worldwide and territorial creation systems. As the growth of tariff activities continues to energize worldwide arrangement vulnerability, the area's speculation possibilities have likewise darkened.

Given the difficult outside condition, policymakers are progressively attempted measures to help momentary development. In recent months, a few national banks in the area have brought down financing costs, including Indonesia, the Philippines, the Republic of Korea, and Thailand. China likewise, as of late acquainted a few changes with its loan fee arrangement, planned for improving the fiscal approach viability and bringing financing costs down to the genuine economy. A couple of nations have likewise declared designs to receive more expansionary financial approaches. In August, Thailand divulged a monetary upgrade bundle of $10 billion (2 percent of the Gross domestic product), which incorporate measures to help ranchers and to support the travel industry area.

South Asia: Covering exchange and political pressures

The worldwide exchange debates cover with political strains and agitated questions in South Asia. The Islamic Republic of Iran remains in a monetary and money emergency amid worldwide political weights that have seriously affected the nation's oil sends out. July evaluations suggest that oil fares could have dropped to as low as 100,000 barrels per day, from practically 2.5 million barrels per day sent out in April 2018—not long before the US withdrew from the atomic arrangement.

Expanded strains between the district's two largest economies, India and Pakistan, have prompted a suspension of reciprocal exchange. Though there is usually little two-sided exchange between the two nations (1–2 percent of all-out fares), the material business in Pakistan depends on imports of synthetic concoctions and cotton from India. Such materials are difficult to substitute in the present moment because of the time required for innovative changes, and the material division would probably experience some transient interruption. In any case, some exchange might be re-directed through Dubai. Assessments propose that backhanded exchange by means of Dubai may as of now be twice as high as the direct two-sided trade. Import tariffs in the U.S; likewise, smallly affect India. Amid the political and exchange pressures, a few nations may profit by shifting exchanging courses and assembling focuses, eminently Bangladesh. The Asian Improvement Bank evaluates that exchange redirection could add around $400 million to stock fares from Bangladesh, and raise Gross domestic product by 0.2 percent. For this, neighboring Myanmar may develop concentrated work assembly.

Western Asia: A year ago's lofty money cheapening is affecting Turkey's exchange execution

In June, Turkey's current record balance enrolled a year moving overflow of $538 million. It is uncommon for Turkey to record a sizeable current record surplus over an entire year. One of the drivers of the nation's quick development since the mid-2000s was considerable outside capital inflows, which financed developing ebb and flow account shortfalls. Be that as it may, since an abrupt stop of remote capital inflows a year ago, the Turkish economy has been attempting to change following another arrangement of macroeconomic limitations. While fixing the household request was required to lessen imports, the precarious cheapening of the Turkish lira was relied upon to build trades amid expanded value intensity. For sure, Turkey's import volumes have shrunk by a normal of 20.3 percent on a year-on-year premise since August 2018, while trade volumes have expanded by 10.6 percent. Over a similar period, the fare unit esteem file has shrunk by a normal of 4.3 percent while the import unit esteem file has scarcely changed. As Turkey's terms-of-exchange have disintegrated since the money debasement, the ascent in send out income is humble comparative with the sizeable increment in trade volumes. Unobtrusive yet strong fare development has been found in the car area, which represents 15 percent in all-out fares. Then, import changes have been gathered in the valuable metal and customer durables divisions.

Latin America and the Caribbean: US China exchange struggle mists the development viewpoint

The US-China exchange strife is burdening the financial viewpoint for Latin America and the Caribbean even as certain nations have seen momentary additions from a preoccupation of exchange streams. Among the area's primary recipients are Brazil's soybean makers and Mexico's apparatus and car divisions. After China forced in July 2018 a 25 percent tariff on soy imports from the US, it progressively went to Brazil to address its issues. China's soybean imports from Brazil rose by 37 percent in 2018, counterbalancing a 50 percent decrease in soybean imports from the US. In the main portion of 2019, be that as it may, a flare-up of African Swine Fever has prompted a sharp drop in China's general interest for soy, which is, to a great extent, utilized for creature feed. Therefore, China's soybean imports from Brazil have additionally fallen. In the interim, Mexico, has profited by an expansion in fares of vehicles, car parts, gadgets and hardware to the US. In these classes, Mexico's piece of the pie in the US has edged up since mid-2018, though China's fell strongly.

Albeit certain segments are picking up from the proceeding with the exchange struggle, the general effect on the locale is probably going to be negative. There are a few channels through which monetary action in Latin America and the Caribbean would be additionally influenced. To start with, China and the US consolidated record for 55 percent of the district's fares. More slow interest development in the two nations would, in this manner, notably affect the locale. Second, the exchange struggle is applying descending weight on product costs, including oil and metals. Toward the beginning of August, copper costs tumbled to the most minimal level in two years, causing send out incomes in Chile and Peru to decrease significantly. Third, the exchange struggle adds to monetary vulnerability, which is as of now raised in a few nations, including Argentina, Brazil, and Mexico, because of local strategy issues. Elevated levels of vulnerability are unfavorably influencing capital streams to the area and speculation, hosing the possibilities for recuperation.

CHINA AND ITS ECONOMIC MUSCLES

Exchange: The yin of China's internationalization methodologies

The most striking aspect of China's internationalization procedures is without question exchange. The quantity of China's biggest organizations on the planet has been growing continuously since 2000, inciting Fortune 500 to discuss the "Chinese Factor" in 2006 (China was then the main nation that had the opportunity to acquire four new organizations into the positioning that year). The quantity of winged serpents keeps on developing. Between 2000 to 2018, their number has been duplicated by ten (going from an unimportant 12 to 120). Meanwhile, the first positioning, the U.S., continues to lose places by more than a third (going from 197 to 126 – just six organizations more than China, anticipating that the Center Realm will overwhelm the positioning in 2019), while the second positioning, Japan also loses half of the spots (going from 103 to 52).

China has likewise begun in a tricky Sun-Tzu style to vanquish the world utilizing its little mythical serpents that have attacked full grown markets, starting with a huge number of little Chinese organizations in Africa and South America that prepare to the greatest ones, supported by the Go Out Arrangement propelled in 1999.

On the whole, the West entered China's market. To be sure, Western organizations (paying little heed to their size) moved their creation in China to appreciate economies of scale and to make sure about portions of the huge household advertise just as to send out their items to the remainder of the world. Chinese organizations' sensu lato then assumed responsibility for the considerably more rewarding neighborhood showcase and have begun attacking the worldwide market. Unquestionably, Chinese organizations attack their household showcase from the start with economies of scale, since the Chinese market itself is immense, something that a Western organization can't bear to do at home from the earliest starting point. A Chinese organization that is rising broadly as of now is a solid organization having prevailed upon a triumph its rivals. It has a solid premise from the beginning in a profoundly divided transitional market with common protectionism that makes the rivalry between Chinese organizations harder and pushes them to preserve and establish a beneficial relationship with the specialists (Guanxi's significance here is indispensable).

A Chinese organization's quality in the neighborhood showcase upsets worldwide rivalry and pulls in Western organizations that propose business understandings. Given the monstrous size of the undiscovered Chinese market, these organizations contend effectively (partly) in the worldwide market and upset the setup request, similar to the case with Haier and Huawei that began clearing Africa, Asia and that has entered Eastern Europe. To do as such, they have the assistance of state coordinations, money related guide, and expense exceptions, a help that is denounced as out of line by Western nations and that must be halted, as expressed by the U.S.

So, the Achilles' impact point of Chinese organizations' contender to internationalization is and remains marking, something that is as yet not yet enormously created in light of China's products notoriety of awful/low quality. Simultaneously, despite the present exchange war, China is sufficiently vigorous to handle what the U.S. is attempting to do with its tariffs since it has built up its New Silk Street (the Belt and Street Activity) weaving its web via land and ocean on three mainlands, yet what helped China's exchange arrive at these statures?

Joint-Adventures: The development motor of the Chinese economy locally and abroad

The development motor of the Chinese economy (particularly at the residential level) is unquestionably joint-adventures (JVs). They are the ideal route for outside endeavors to work together, ensured by the Chinese state. With about 20,000 remote organizations settling in China yearly since 1978, the all-out speculation volume is presently more than 100 billion, making China the world's plant, creating in huge amounts requiring little to no effort to the point of turning into the focal point of the planet's endemic development.

The changes raised monetary effectiveness by acquainting benefit motivators with provincial aggregate undertakings (which are owned by the nearby government but are controlled by advertising standards), family cultivates, little private organizations, and outside financial specialists and merchants. They also liberated numerous undertakings from steady mediation by state specialists. Therefore, somewhere in the

1978 and 1992 period, the yield of state-claimed undertakings declined from 56 percent of national yield to 40 percent, while the portion of aggregate endeavors increased from 42 to 50 percent and that of private organizations and joint endeavors increased from 2 to 10 percent. The benefit impetuses seem to have had a further constructive outcome in the private capital market, as processing plant proprietors and little makers anxious to build benefits (they could keep a greater amount of them) are gradually dedicating more of their organizations' own incomes to enhancing business execution.

China's ongoing profitability execution is astounding. By correlation, profitability development for the Asian tigers drifted around 2 percent, at times marginally more, for the 1966-91 period. China's pace of very nearly 4 percent places it in a class without anyone else.

Why the Efficiency Blast?

Precisely how did the financial changes in China work to help efficiency, particularly in an economy given all that was troubled by broad government controls? In a significant country segment, the story is especially intriguing.

Nearly four out of every five Chinese worked in horticulture before the 1978 changes; by 1994, only one out of two did. Changes extended property rights in the open country and ignited a race to shape little non-agricultural organizations in provincial territories. Additionally, decollectivization and more expenditure on agrarian items prompted progressively profitable (family) ranches and increasingly effective utilization of work. These powers together initiated numerous laborers to move out of agribusiness. The resulting rapid growth of town endeavors has drawn a huge number of individuals from conventional horticulture into higher-esteem included assembling.

Further, the post-1978 changes conceded more noteworthy self-governance to big business chiefs. They turned out to be all the more allowed to set their own creation objectives, sell a few items in the private market at serious costs, award rewards to great specialists and fire awful ones, and hold some bit of the company's profit for future venture. The changes likewise gave more prominent space for private responsibility for, and these secretly held organizations made occupations, grew much-needed customer items, earned significant hard cash through the remote exchange, made good on state burdens, and gave the national economy adaptability and versatility that it had previously failed to have.

By inviting remote speculation, China's open-entryway strategy has added capacity to the monetary change. Aggregate outside direct speculation, immaterial before 1978, came to about US$100 billion of every 1994; yearly inflows expanded from under 1 percent of the absolute fixed interest in 1979 to 18 percent in 1994. This remote cash has constructed industrial facilities, made employments, connected China to universal markets, and prompted significant exchanges of innovation. These patterns are particularly clear in the more than one dozen open beach front regions where outside speculators appreciate favorable charge circumstances. Likewise, monetary progression has supported fares - which rose 19 percent a year during 1981-94. The solid fare development, thus, seems to have stimulated the development of profitability in residential enterprises.

In one last zone, value change, the Chinese have continued warily, allowing a decent lot of self-sufficiency to makers of shopper merchandise and horticultural items yet significantly less to different parts. Over the last two decades, a few episodes of development slammed the Chinese economy, deflecting the administration from carrying out full-scale value advancement. High paces of development likewise raise inflationary concerns. Swelling may represent the single most prominent danger to Chinese development; however, it has been largely confined up to this point.

A More Top to bottom Look

Similarly, as with any national economy, China has novel attributes that the specialist should appropriately represent.

To begin with, numerous analysts refer to the intermittent political emergencies that held onto China before 1978 as a factor darkening pre-1978 monetary quality. Since the political atmosphere in China was such a great amount in transition, these observers contend, the monetary pictures when 1978 can't be contrasted and any exactness. This suggestion was assessed by dropping from the examination of the 1958-70 subperiod, which includes the Incomparable Jump Forward and the Social Unrest. The outcome is that pre-1978 efficiency has, therefore, expanded just unassumingly from 1.1 to 1.6 percent.

Second, in the 1953-78 time frame, Chinese focal organizers put intensely in the modern urban area and limited movement from the nation into the urban areas. Could the deserting of this approach after 1978 clarify the solid execution of the economy? Did these sectoral shifts drive development, or did efficiency? In the occasion, in spite of the fact that these sectoral shifts are significant, they don't dispose of the free ascent in profitability related to the changes.

Third, a few observers keep up that if the profitability development was a one-time shot of adrenaline to the body monetary, it is not economical. Truth be told, profitability gains have been consistent across 1979-94 and even expanded during 1990-94. If the post-change period is broken into three particular stages, each related to a different arrangement of changes, sizable profitability gains are obvious in each subperiod. This shows that the Chinese had the option to extend introductory efficiency additions to different pieces of the economy.

At last, one can examine the investigation for estimation issues. Specifically, are the capital-stock information determined appropriately, and were there any estimation blunders identifying with the information? As regards the capital-stock estimation, since the Chinese national salary insights prohibit the estimation of private lodging and since expenses for new lodging increased during 1978-94, the venture figures ought to be balanced in the same way. At the point when this is done, there is no change to the pre-1978 profitability development gauge and an unassuming increment in the post-change efficiency development rate, which confirms the general story. Could an overvaluation of the underlying capital stock have one-sided the discoveries? Progressively traditionalist appraisals of the capital stock were utilized to re-examine the information, but there is no solid proof to invalidate the findings. Given the fact that the pre-

1978 profitability picks up become negative, the rate of post-change efficiency remains unchanged.

Another growing issue with capital-stock information is that Chinese resource reviews do not consistently deliver capital stock evaluations with the speculation information in the national records. The difficulties in crossing this factual hole are extensive. The investigative discoveries of this examination were contrasted and those acquired by market analysts who had registered the information differently to some degree. On the efficiency side, the investigations differed in accentuation, however, not generally: as a body, the accessible proof validates profitability upgrades as a significant wellspring of post-1978 development, in any event, when different capital-stock computations are utilized. The outside evaluations of profitability development change from around 2 percent to about 4 percent for the 1979-94 period.

Concerning input information, an investigation was made of the potential for a differential inclination that may exaggerate the post-change development comparative with the pre-change period. This issue may emerge in view of the fact that halfway arranged economies are likely to yield overreporting and cost-discounting. As it occurs, in spite of the fact that endeavor chiefs have generally tended to overreport yield with an end goal of reaching creation targets set by the administration, the motivating forces to do so have presumably declined in the change period as directors have confronted less severe state control. In this way, it is far-fetched that the exhibition was exaggerated in the post-1978 period compared to before.

The underdeflating of ostensible yield could be an increasingly genuine wellspring of predisposition. The piecemeal character of value change - with certain divisions changed and others not- - implies that choosing a suitable deflator for the post-1978 period is difficult. However, the central planning period may also have seen an underdeflation of output, since repressed inflation was probably widespread (as manifested in shortages, black market trading, and long waits for certain goods). Thus, the measurement problem, while real, probably does not much alter the basic conclusion about substantial productivity gains after 1978.

IMPACTS OF THE EMERGENCY ON THE CREATING AND CHANGE NATIONS

The emergency started in the major money related focuses on the created nations. The power of effect on creating and change nations became evident just bit by bit. The circumstance is new; past emergencies spread from the creating nations. This time creating nations are the casualties of the emergency; however, they didn't cause it. "The reasons for the worldwide budgetary emergency are to be found in the monetary and financial arrangements of the created nations, basically the (US). Creating nations are not liable for it, yet they are presently truly influenced," composed Martin Khor, the new Executive of the South Place in Geneva.1

The Third World System (2008) detailed that the UN Monetary Commission for Asia and the Pacific had, in reality, enlisted a "period of uplifted unsteadiness." However, around then, they diminished their development forecasts just negligibly. In the IMF July 2008 update of the Worldwide Money related Steadiness Report (IMF GFSR)2, the IMF, as far as it matters for its, enlisted a debilitating of development in the limited nations and an increased danger of expansion. Acquiring abroad turned out to be increasingly costly; speculators had become more hazard cognizant. Be that as it may, the IMF, despite everything, portrayed the edge nations as decently emergency safe. The full power of the worldwide money related and financial emergency affected the creating and edge nations throughout 2008. Along these lines, the IMF, the World Bank, and different foundations consistently minimized their development expectations for Asia, Latin America, or more all Africa.3 High development rates vanished, and numerous nations even needed to endure contracting financial production.

According to the IMF April 2009 World Monetary Viewpoint (IMF WEO), the development misfortunes in the edge and creating nations were higher than in the industrialized nations. Contrasted and their development potential, the creating and limit nations are along these lines harder hit by the worldwide budgetary and financial emergency than the industrialized nations that caused it.

The relapse in monetary development involved a sinking for each capita pay, at any rate in nations with high populace development rates. Large scale monetarily the emergency manifested itself in mounting deficiencies in exchange and installment adjusts, lessening money saves, cash debasements, expanding paces of expansion, higher obligation and taking off open spending shortfalls

This directly affected the everyday environments of the populace. The Assembled Countries Instructive, Scientific and Social Association (UNESCO) (2009), evaluated that the fall in development cost the 390 million most unfortunate individuals in Africa. For example, the individuals who must get by on what might be compared to USD 1 every day, an aggregate of some USD 18 billion or USD 46 for each individual. For every one-fifth capita salary, this is proportionate to a fall in normal. The Worldwide Job Association (ILO) (2008) predicted that the number of unemployed could grow to 50 million somewhere before the end of 2009. The unevenness is mounting. Without further ado before the G-20 gathering in Washington in November 2008, the World Bank assessed that a fall in development of 1% would compel 20 million individuals into supreme destitution (World Bank 2008). A half-year later, the World Bank anticipated that the quantity of poor would rise further down the middle of the creating nations. Among the low-pay nations upwards of 33% and in the nations south of the Sahara upwards of seventy-five percent would be influenced (World Bank GMR 2009). This implies the Thousand years of Advancement Objectives blurred into the separation for some nations. As an outcome, there has just been social distress in some countries.4 In its most recent yearbook, the universal system Social Watch (2009) reports, in various commitments by neighborhood common society associations, on how the emergency has emotionally affected individual nations.

Emergency transmission channels

The emergency didn't affect all locales, nations, and populace bunches similarly or on a similar time scale. The examples grew differently for every nation. Then again, the transmission channel designs are clear (Te Velde 2008; IDS 2008; Toporowski 2009). The money related and monetary emergency of the industrialized States spread to the creating nations fundamentally utilizing budgetary streams and through the exchange. The closer a creating nation is combined with the worldwide economy, the more grounded and increasingly quick the effect of the emergency.

Transmission through money related streams

10Obviously the breakdown of the stock trades in the incredible fund communities in May 2008 was likewise immediately transmitted to the stock trades in the most significant rising nations. The stock trades in China, India, Russia, South Africa, and Brazil, for instance, took action accordingly right away. Inside seven days, the Morgan Stanley Capital Global Developing Business sector Record, which mirrors the securities exchanges in the edge nations, fell by 23%. It is normal for these nations that they, as of now, have a profoundly evolved fund part that is combined with different nations. The more fragile the guidelines in the nation, the more defenseless it is to chance.

Particularly seriously affected were the nations whose Sovereign Riches Assets had been put resources into poisonous, presently definitely depreciated qualities, for example, Singapore and the oil-delivering States in the Center East. Securities exchange misfortunes additionally sharply affected nations like Chile, whose annuity reserves incorporate offers from the industrialized nations.

Net capital streams to the creating nations sank forcefully. As per the World Bank, capital streams to the creating nations dropped to USD 727 billion out of 2008. They had added up to nearly USD 1,160 billion in the previous year (see table 1). The World Bank and the IMF are expecting a decline to this year. The Global Finance Foundation reported the opposite and expected flow of capital in the current year in energetically developing markets (28 limit nations) of USD 141 billion in June 2009, not quite a large portion of the 2008 figure (USD 392 billion) and only one-fifth of the 2007 stream that accumulated to USD 888 billion (IIF 2009). Most importantly, the nations in Eastern Europe, and especially Russia and Ukraine, have been hit especially hard. The withdrawal of outside capital prompted cheapening of monetary standards in the creating nations.

Consequently not exclusively were the progressions of portfolio and direct ventures to the creating nations significantly lower, yet business bank credits and non-bank financing were additionally decreased. As to coordinate speculation (FDI) in the creating nations, the Unified Countries Meeting on Exchange and Improvement (UNCTAD) posted a frail development of 7% on a sinking bend for 2008. The growth was already as high as 21 percent in 2007 (UNCTAD 2009). For the principal quarter of 2009, UNCTAD predicts that the FDI will fall by 25% in the creating nations and by 40% in the change nations. Financial specialists moved their assets to as far as anyone knows lower-chance nations. More unfortunate monetary possibilities kept speculation designs down. Arranged takeovers5 were delayed or revoked. The credit crunch rendered the financing of such activities progressively difficult.

The worldwide banks, as of now, encountering difficulties conceded less and less credit to creating and edge nations. In 2009 there was even a net withdrawal of credits. Towards the finish of 2008, taking up credits by governments and private ventures in creating nations was for all intents and purposes at a stop. There was a remarkable ascent in hazard premiums and paces of enthusiasm for creating nations on the security markets. During the initial nine months of 2008, Brazil encountered a capital channel of USD 13 billion, Argentina

USD 20 billion, Mexico, and Venezuela USD 19 billion each.6 At long last, credit business was ended where assets had been acquired at low rates, for example in Japan or Switzerland, and put resources into high-intrigue nations ("convey exchange ").

In various nations, settlements by transients which had constantly been rising as of late deteriorated or even sank. Nations that were especially hard hit by the scale of settlements in the capital stream, such as the Focal American States and India (World Bank 2009; Awad 2009; Burki and Mordasini 2009). The stop or the opposite in settlements has also been paired with a freeze in remote work commitments or even the repatriation of outside workers.7

Finally, there is a danger of relapse or possibly stagnation in authentic advancement help (ODA). In any case, for the year 2008, the Association for Monetary Co-activity and Improvement (OECD) detailed an ascent in ODA contributed by part nations to 0.3% of the gross national salary (GNI) (OECD 2009). As indicated by OECD, should the quantitative targets set for 2010 be accomplished, the part nations would need to expand their guide even further.8 During past emergencies, the benefactor States constantly diminished their guide. Giver States with significant spending deficiencies and mounting open obligation minimize the need for advancement aid.9 This would apply pressure most importantly on those creating nations where ODA represents a high extent of approaching capital

Transmission by means of exchange

On record of the world monetary downturn, there was a sharp fall in the interest for products and ventures from the creating and developing nations. The fall in development in China and India additionally involved a drop in their interest for vitality and mineral crude materials, especially from Africa. Sinking costs and fare volumes prompted a breakdown in send out salary (UNCTAD 2009c). The 49 most unfortunate creating nations saw their fare pay marked down by 43.8% during the first half-year of 2009.10 The more significant the creating nation fares to the US, Europe or the bigger limit nations, or the more prominent pay adaptability of the costs of fare merchandise, the more grounded the effect on the nation's fares. Taking into account its closeness to the US, Mexico is a significant model. The Bangladeshi month to month development rates for material fares diminished until April 2009; from that point forward they have been negative. In July 2009 Bangladesh sent out 10%, not exactly around the same time the earlier year. In Kenya, the national bank cautioned of a fall in fares of blossoms. In Zambia, send out profit for copper slammed by 54% during the primary quarter of 2009. The traveler goals in the Caribbean and Africa were confronted with droops in salary. The higher the extent of fares in the total national output (Gross domestic product) of a nation, the harder the effect of decreasing interest during an emergency. A nation where a solitary division represents a high extent of the economy was especially defenseless to a clustering hazard, as on account of the Slovak Republic with its car industry and Ukraine with its steel industry.

Lower State salary may likewise be combined with sinking send out pay, as on account of Côte d'Ivoire, Lesotho, and Swaziland, where 40-half of State pay gets from customs obligations (IMF 2009e).

Reactions to the emergency

In the affluent nations, the conversation on the most proficient method to manage the worldwide money related and monetary emergency minimized the creating nations and their needs. On all occasions, the effect of the emergency on the developing nations didn't hit the features the way bank bailouts and poisonous protections did.

In ongoing years, many creating nations have gained significant large scale monetary ground. This way, some of them are preferred furnished against the emergency regarding they were on past events. These nations are not presented to the emergency with no insurance, whatever. Numerous administrations in the creating nations have embraced measures as per their own forces. They have strengthened their (territorial) collaboration with each other. The UN, IMF, World Bank, and other worldwide associations have likewise tried to help creating nations. They were encouraged to act by the non-legislative associations and various scholastic forces.

Building up nations' reaction at the national level

21There is a significant level of variety in the underlying situation of the individual creating nations. Some have high worldwide cash holds. Others have a generous inland market. Notwithstanding, numerous nations had just been seriously drained by the nourishment and vitality emergencies.

Different models are Korea, Malaysia, the Philippines, Thailand, and Vietnam. South Africa likewise stepp (...)

22Wealthy nations reacted with broad monetary interventions.11 Various creating nations also propelled projects of this sort. Nations with significant universal cash saves and a low spending shortfall, similar to China, were in a situation to do as such. China declared a CNY 4 billion program (some EUR 430 billion) for the years 2009 and 2010 to be put resources into a residential framework. The government managed savings, innovation, condition, and education. Ortiz posted an investigation of monetary incitement designs in 43 industrialized and creating nations according to Walk 2009 (Ortiz 2009). Be that as it may, a technique dependent on singular projects for every nation was viewed as lacking, and a multilateral, facilitated approach was called for. Most of the creating nations had and still have a distinctly lower monetary, political degree for projects of incitement and social initiatives to secure the least fortunate ones. Utilizing an uncommon monetary limit marker, a UNESCO group learned that 43 of the 48 low-pay nations inspected have no degree for incitement bundles for poor people (UNESCO 2009). Higher reciprocal guide and liquidity help from the global financing establishments could significantly grow the scope of alternatives for such nations.

Other nations, similar to India, selected different ways. India has significant worldwide cash stores to approach. However, it additionally has high financial shortfalls, which pretty much rule out expanded consumption. Subsequently, India put the accentuation on financial measures, specifically encouraging credit to get to alternatives for makers. In certain creating nations, be that as it may, these cash arrangement measures are carefully constrained because easement in premium approach impacts the conversion standard of their money and the pace of swelling.

Conversely, the impact of cheapening of monetary standards as a specific fare motivator measure would likely be constrained as long as worldwide interest didn't rise all the more unequivocally. A few nations, interestingly, have presented particular exchange limitations on superfluous extravagance products.

More grounded South-South participation

There are not really any dependable figures accessible so far on the impacts of the emergency on South-South exchange and South-South direct speculation. The articulated development of past years will be to some degree eased back however will keep, as per Khalil Hamdani, Exceptional Counsel of the South Place in Geneva (Hamdani 2009).

China additionally made two-sided money related swaps in the billions to, among others, Korea, Hong Kong, Indon (...)

A genuine case of strengthened South-South collaboration is the extension of the Relationship of South-East Asian Countries (ASEAN) multilateral credit understanding. In February 2009 the money pastors of these nations in addition to China, Japan and Korea raised the extent of this Chiang Mai Activity to USD 120 billion (ASEAN 2009).13

Argentina, Bolivia, Brazil, Ecuador, Paraguay, Uruguay and Venezuela. See likewise Agencia de Prensa d (...)

In May 2009, seven South American States14 established the Bank of the South with a cash-flow to be paid in of USD 7 billion to back advancement ventures. Likewise, being talked about is an extension on the lines of a money related association or a fiscal adjustment subsidize (Ugarteche and

Ortiz 2009). In April 2008 the Bolivarian Union for the Americas gathering of Latin American States settled on a joint fiscal committee, reference money for their between State exchange, a chamber for installment payments and a save subsidize for exchange exchanges (Cassen 2008).

The creator makes reference to Japan, the Unified Realm and the European Association (EU). In any case, she additionally calls for (...)

Morais de Sa e Silva sees a specific threat for South-South collaboration (Morais de Sa e Silva 2009). South-South activities are in effect progressively supported by ODA.15 Such triangular tasks could succumb to decreased ODA.

Worldwide activities

The same ever-repeating subjects run like a red string through the worldwide activities to manage money related and financial emergencies, despite the fact that they might be weighted differently or even run the restricting way. It is constantly an issue of the change of the global money related framework, obtaining of extra liquidity, control and guideline of business sectors and the specific abilities of a wide scope of foundations.

The essential entertainers for advancement approach discusses were the UN and sure of their uncommon associations, the Bretton Woods establishments, the EU and the territorial improvement banks. The G-20 expected an incontestable job. Non-administrative associations all through the world had a functioning influence in these conversations and distributed various archives. Numerous in the scholarly world were worried about these issues.

The UN guaranteed a significant job for itself at an early point. UN Secretary General Boycott Ki-Moon had offered to have a worldwide gathering on the money related emergency. He got the sponsorship of the Gathering of 77 (G-77) and numerous common society associations. Futile! The UN and its sub-associations put ahead investigations, arranged meetings, classes, and proposed measures. Yet, the more significant job tumbled to the G-20 and the Bretton Woods foundations.

Terroristic assaults

1. Direct Monetary Demolition

The quickest and quantifiable effect of fear-mongering is physical devastation. Fear-based oppressors crush existing plants, machines, transportation frameworks, laborers, and other financial assets. For littler scopes, demonstrations of psychological oppression may explode bistros, holy places, or streets. Huge scope assaults, most scandalously the World Exchange Community bombings on Sept. 11, 2001, can pulverize billions of dollars' worth of property and pointlessly murder a huge number of gainful workers.3

The effect of fear-based oppression and war is constant negative for the economy, and physical annihilation is a huge motivation behind why. Profitable assets that could have produced important merchandise and enterprises are annihilated, while different assets are perpetually occupied from other beneficial uses to reinforce the military and guard. None of this makes riches or adds to the way of life, despite the fact that military spending is often incorrectly referred to as an energizer; this is the "broken window false notion" now and then referenced by economists.

2. Expanded Vulnerability in the Business sectors

Regardless of whether you don't live anyplace approach to psychological militant assaults, you may, at present, be contrarily affected in a roundabout way. This is on the grounds that a wide range of business sectors despise vulnerability, and fear-mongering does a lot of that. The monetary markets were shut down after Sept. 11 and didn't generally recuperate until months after 2003. There is much debate about the profundity and inescapability of the real effect on monetary markets. While the dangers and exposure of psychological oppression worldwide continue to increase, markets give off an illusion that they are becoming increasingly versatile. Financial exchange records didn't decrease a lot after the fear monger assaults in France killed in any event 129 individuals in 2015.65 Nonetheless, the lethal assault in Decent, France. In 2016, it only added to the slant that France might be an inexorably temperamental spot to live and work together in. The genuine risk of worldwide psychological warfare from a speculator's viewpoint is about the more extensive picture, not singular occurrences. Universal speculation and collaboration are lower in a world loaded with psychological warfare.

3. Protection, Exchange, The travel industry, and FDI

There are two evident enterprises particularly defenseless against the impacts of fear-based oppression: protection and the travel industry. Not all insurance agencies payout in case of worldwide fear mongering or remote wars, so the effect is likely short of what you may initially anticipate. In any case, fear-based oppression is an unsafe business for everybody, and insurance agencies abhor chance as much as any other individual.

The travel industry is much all the more concerning. In France, for instance, the travel industry represents around 7% to 8% of all-out total national output (GDP).7 Vanguelis Panayotis, a chief of MKG the travel industry consultancy, disclosed to Reuters that he anticipated that a 30% decrease in guests should France in the month after the Decent attacks.8

On a more extensive scale, fear-based oppression harms global exchange. This might be because of unavoidable dangers, for example, bargained exchange courses and dissemination frameworks, or as a result of the mental and physical responses to fear-based oppression. This additionally implies less remote direct venture (FDI), particularly in precarious nations.

4. War Is the Soundness of the State

There is a well-known adage in the investigation of political economy that peruses "war is the soundness of the state." It implies that during times of contention, receptive governments and anxious residents are unquestionably progressively slanted to surrender financial and political opportunities in return for security.10 This may lead to higher duties, higher government shortages, and higher swelling. The legislature also implements value controls during wartime, even the nationalization of ventures.

Governments are less viable at overseeing assets for gainful financial action than private people, particularly when those assets are co-picked to accomplish a vital military target. At the point when governments mobilize, the private economy endures. As a financial specialist and student of history, Robert Higgs showed in his book "Emergency and Leviathan," numerous administration controls remain set up long after military battles end.11

5. Expanded Patriotism and Outside Wariness

The last hazard to the economy is a political hazard. This is as of now in plain view in the US and Europe in 2016, where there has been an ascent in doubt of remote societies, organizations, migrant laborers, and displaced people. Populist developments previously won a triumph of sorts in the Assembled Realm, where hostile to globalist and against exchange notions helped pass Brexit. These sorts of major political occasions have an unsure financial aftermath on everything from cash to exchange and tact.

Shutting down outskirts to exchange and settler laborers reduces the size and decent variety of financial exchanges and cutoff points profitable assets. Business analysts as ahead of schedule as Adam Smith battled that the division of work and gains from exchange are restricted to the size of accessible components of production.12 Similarly, as a solitary family or town, it is less beneficial if it depends on inner assets, so too do national economies confined to the degree to which they divide off outer makers and shoppers.

Coronavirus pandemic

The effect of the improvement of the Covid-19 Coronavirus pandemic on the worldwide economy will be exceptionally enormous. The worldwide economy is compromised by a downturn in 2020. Emergency interventionist financial approach programs are expected to run. I depicted these issues on my RG profile. Not many monetary elements, for example, pharmaceutical organizations that will make an antibody for Coronavirus Covid-19 or ventures creating disinfectants, defensive covers, sterile gloves, and so forth. In any case, there will be a lot more ventures, parts of the economy as well as organizations and endeavors that will see reductions in incomes from the offer made of items and administrations advertised. In macroeconomic terms, nations that are exporters of certain crude materials with as of now low-value levels on product trades will endure progressively monetary and money related misfortunes. In meso-financial terms, the travel industry, transport, neighborliness, gastronomy, the big time, social occasions, and related administrations will suffer enormous misfortunes and areas. In microeconomic terms, falling different deals will likewise be noted by numerous different endeavors from different ventures and parts that are cooperatives of different undertakings working in enterprises portrayed by falling gainfulness.

The SARS-Cov-2 Coronavirus pandemic is as yet creating in numerous nations. In numerous nations, there has been a suggestion or legitimate commitment: If you can remain at home. For some nations, the SARS-Cov-2 Coronavirus pandemic is just in the early periods of a pestilence. Coronavirus pandemic is a worldwide epidemic as of now. Any individual who can stay at home to diminish the danger of a pandemic spreading. Everybody who can change to remote correspondence, for example, using the Web and phone. It is likewise important to advance just dependable data, for example, completely affirmed by scientific research in the field of virology.

The Coronavirus has just started to evolve, new strains of the Coronavirus are framing, which may frustrate the rapid progress of immunization or other remedial treatment, and the issue of negative economic effects may persist for a longer period. Do any of you have solid information sources affirming this kind of data that is now showing up in different authority media?

Considering the abovementioned, scientific research shows that seclusion is presently the best preventive arrangement on the grounds that Coronavirus is portrayed by significant levels of disease, and there is no antibody or some other completely successful medication for Coronavirus yet. Furthermore, it is assessed that numerous individuals who do not have illness side effects do not become ill. Yet, they may, as of now, be tainted with Coronavirus, so the pandemic doesn't grow, all individuals ought to follow the suggestions, for example, you should wash your hands often, remain at home and cut off the exit from home to the important least. Individuals who show any side effects of a cool, for example, a runny nose or hack, ought not to go out on the grounds that they might be tainted with Coronavirus, despite the fact that they are not truly sick. The thought is to limit the degree of the spread of the Coronavirus pandemic. At present, separation, home isolate is the best answer for all individuals, whether or not they are debilitated or not.

The significance of web advertising has been developing as of late, remembering the utilization of internet-based life gateways for advancement and promotion. This significance is especially expanding with regard to the current Coronavirus pandemic. As of now, the utilization of new online media has especially constructive angles if youngsters use cell phones to get the vital, significant, and solid data and utilize web-based life entrances at work and in training forms when numerous work environments, schools, and colleges have suspended their exercises. Right now, the significance of utilizing new online media for correspondence and training in the advancement of the Coronavirus pandemic is developing significantly. In light of the improvement of the Coronavirus pandemic in numerous nations, schools (right now near Walk 2020) are shutting for 2-3 weeks, youngsters with instructors and should get in touch with one another just remotely by means of the Web.

In my nation, kindergartens, schools, and universities are officially shut down for about fourteen days. I noticed that schools and universities were even shut down in some different nations to restrict the progress of the pestilence. I agree this is the best approach due to the high probability of possibly plague spread. Young people typically don't have a coronavirus. Still, they can pass Coronavirus and contaminate others without much of a break, so shutting schools and universities is a preventive and genuine measure. At the point when schools and colleges are shut, e-learning training ought to proceed. The utilization of ICTs in training is now developing. In my nation, the conclusion of schools and universities isn't treated as an extra get-away. The administration suggests that kids and youngsters remain at home and study at home.

Questions emerge about the hazard relationship of the degree of infectiousness and the death pace of Coronavirus contrasted with different illnesses and maladies that cause high mortality. Different infections, including those brought about by taking paper-like energizers, liquor, and so on., diabetes, atherosclerosis, and so on, are now notable. It is clear how to treat these ailments and so forth. Coronavirus is as yet a major puzzle. The size of the conceivable advancement of a pandemic is obscure. Coronavirus has an elevated level of disease, and there is no immunization or some other completely successful Coronavirus sedate yet.

What's more, it is evaluated that numerous individuals who don't have indications don't become ill, yet they may, as of now, be contaminated with Coronavirus. Also, it has now turned out (mid-Walk 2020) that Coronavirus is quickly transforming, new assortments are rising, so controlling a pandemic will be extremely difficult. The issue of a pandemic may, in any case, create in numerous nations for at least half a month or months. It is at present the greatest clinical, wellbeing, financial issue, and so forth.

At present, be that as it may, it is difficult to anticipate what the world will resemble once humankind has tackled the Coronavirus issue. A great deal will change without a doubt, and the economy will appear to be unique. In order to endure this difficult time of monetary downturn, numerous endeavors will be compelled to do hierarchical, innovative, budgetary, and other rebuilding forms. We would already be able to see numerous changes. The economy, individuals' conduct, nourishment inclinations, lifestyle, types of work are evolving, and so forth. The significance of remote work and learning using the Web is expanding. Shopper inclinations and buying profiles of residents will change. We would already be able to see that numerous individuals, dreading for their wellbeing, change their dietary patterns, and pick solid natural nourishment. Smokers are thinking about stopping smoking from expanding their body's protection from different infection assaults. A great deal will change, yet we don't have the foggiest idea how much, because there is no response to numerous inquiries concerning the potential for the continuation of the scourge, presently the Coronavirus pandemic. We don't have the foggiest idea when the antibody will be developed? Possibly just in a couple of months or later. These are the evaluations of pharmaceutical organizations. We don't know whether the Coronavirus infection will transform and make its new, similarly risky assortments. There are many question marks. What is sure is that after the Coronavirus period, the world will appear to be unique. The economy and life of numerous individuals will unquestionably change a great deal, yet we don't have the foggiest idea how much and how the world will look like after the Coronavirus period.

Numerous inquiries have yet to be addressed in the coming days or sometimes based on scientific study in the not too distant future. For example, it is now known that Coronavirus will persist for up to 3-4 days on objects (with smooth surfaces, for example, shopping baskets). It is subsequently important to take unusual account in contacts under various circumstances. You can always wash your hands with the use of cleansers that separate the Coronavirus. It is likewise realized that Coronavirus is tragically impervious to slight temperature changes. As indicated by the World Wellbeing Association, the appearance of spring and summer (in 2020 in the northern half of the globe of the planet Earth), raising the air temperature by up to twelve degrees C won't cause the Coronavirus to separate. We definitely know a great deal, yet we don't know more. It is important to proceed with scientific research in the field of Coronavirus infectivity and potential strategies for controlling Coronavirus, and so on.

Then again, it is sure that the Coronavirus pandemic will enormously influence the worldwide economy. Because of the advancement of the coronavirus pandemic, the downturn of the worldwide economy is conceivable in 2020. In numerous nations now (mid-Walk 2020), the extra enemy of emergency, ace turn of events, actuating enterprise, utilization, bank loaning proportions of financial, budgetary, and money related arrangement instruments are propelled. Today, numerous market analysts and monetary examiners state that there will be a downturn in numerous nations where the travel industry is one of the primary parts of the economy. Unquestionably Coronavirus' effect on the economy, money related markets, and the vitality area will be exceptionally enormous. Since the costs of stocks, gold, vitality assets, and different resources on capital markets are falling quickly, the size of the financial stoppage in numerous nations will positively be with regards to the high danger of a worldwide economic downturn in 2020. The accompanying inquiry presently emerges: Is a significant decrease in loan costs a decent enemy of an emergency instrument, because of which the world can stay away from the worldwide economic downturn in 2020? Tragically, an ever-increasing number of monetary information shows that the current (mid-Walk 2020) improvement of the Coronavirus pandemic may prompt a worldwide downturn in 2020. There will unquestionably be a downturn in numerous nations where the travel industry is one of the primary parts of the economy. Unquestionably Coronavirus' effect on the economy, money related markets, and the vitality area will be exceptionally enormous. The costs of stocks, gold, vitality assets, and different resources on capital markets are quickly falling. We at present have a securities exchange crash on the financial exchange like other financial exchange crashes that have recently begun worldwide budgetary and/or monetary emergencies. Taking into account the abovementioned, the downturn of the worldwide economy in 2020 is likely. In like manner, national banks are expanding their movement to keep up liquidity in the financial divisions. Be that as it may, just some national banks have chosen to bring down financing costs. Should different banks take comparable activities? Should national banks significantly lower financing costs as interventionist hostile to emergency measures? Can a significant decrease in financing costs, bringing loan costs down to levels near zero or beneath zero, to levels of negative loan fees be a decent enemy of emergency instrument? Will bringing financing costs down to negative loan fees increment liquidity and permit loaning in banking areas to be kept up at ideal levels? Is a significant decrease in loan costs a decent enemy of an emergency instrument, on account of which the world can evade the downturn of the worldwide economy in 2020?

As I would like to think, against emergency estimates that have been executed in many nations since pre-winter 2008 as a major aspect of interventionist, Keynsian, hostile to emergency financial and money related approach has ended up being generally powerful. After a long time of utilization, the economies of numerous nations returned to adjust and financial development. In 2020, the worldwide economy, because of the improvement of the Coronavirus pandemic, is compromised by a downturn, a solid decrease in monetary development, an expansion in joblessness, abatement underway, speculation, a lessening in charge incomes to the open money framework, and so on. Subsequently, in 2020 comparative moves ought to likewise be made under interventionist, Keynsian, against emergency financial strategy and fiscal arrangements, like those enemies of emergency and advancement situated exercises that have been done since harvest time 2008 for a time of quite a long while. Exercises that under interventionist, Keynsian, hostile to emergency financial approach and fiscal arrangement, like those enemies of emergency and advancement situated estimates that have been actualized since harvest time 2008, should now be taken and created in my productions accessible on the Exploration Door site.

In my nation, as in many different nations, the legislature is currently taking a shot at building up an enemy of an emergency procedure, a Keynesian financial strategy during the Coronavirus pandemic, for example, the meaning of instruments for monetary and budgetary star improvement approach, whose errand will be to animate business enterprise in case of an intense decrease in financial development brought about by advancement Coronavirus pandemic. Simultaneously, focal banking, hypothetically autonomous of the legislature (however just hypothetically), is thinking about bringing down loan fees and propelling a program to purchase Treasury securities on the optional market to build liquidity in the open money segment. Likewise, the national bank may dispatch credits for business puts money on special terms and/or acquisition of lost cases, for example, unpaid advances and garbage protections. Business banks, which in my nation are at present generally under state control (the Treasury controls a significant piece of the financial division), dispatch a program of conceding reimbursement of bank advances (essentially home loan and business) offered to borrowers (for the most part home loan and business) at no extra expense. Be that as it may, because, in the period of the structure and usage of hostile to emergency financial approach in the time of the Coronavirus pandemic, governmental issues instead of logic commands to an enormous degree, the issue of the viability of executing against emergency financial strategy is sketchy. Remarks from different political circles proposing totally opposing ideas for hostile to emergency financial approach show up in the media. A few media consider issues, for example, regardless of whether the national bank ought to or ought not to begin purchasing obligations in danger from high credit hazard from general society and/or business money related division. Conclusions that are totally opposing are distributed in the media without directing an open, considerable discussion. Specialists in the field of hostile to emergency, Keynesian financial approach provide prepared answers for the developing emergency circumstance. Be that as it may, for certain worlds of politics, consistent question and steady analysis is a higher priority than collaborating during this specific time of advancement of the Coronavirus pandemic and working together to find the best enemy of emergency, Keynesian financial strategy. The present time frame is exceptional.

The creating monetary emergency is significantly different from the worldwide budgetary emergency of 2008. the determined log jam in monetary development in 2020 will be produced for the most part by a lessening in liquidity in open money related divisions and not a diminishing in liquidity in business budgetary areas, for example, the circumstance known from harvest time 2008. The fundamental inquiry presently is: How with what ventures should extra cash be brought into the economy so this additional cash makes new openings and interests in the genuine economy? Nations with their cash are currently considering a significant increment in the size of extra cash supply to the economy. Further inquiries: Which adventures in the open part and the business division ought to be coordinated towards extra cash with the goal that genuine, new undertakings, new openings and so forth are made rather than only or predominantly supporting current utilization and checking the drop in the valuation of protections on stock trades? Obviously, issues such as supporting current use and balancing declines in the valuation of protections on stock trades are equally significant. Still, for a while, these exercises alone do not regularly mean reasonable monetary development in the real economy. No one can tell precisely how solid the fall in financial development will be, how severe the downturn in the world economy will be due to the advance of the Coronavirus pandemic. Therefore, presently in this specific period, rather than directing questions for the most part dictated by political intentions, every single political hover, together with specialists, autonomous market analysts work in the field of hostile to an emergency, the Keynesian financial strategy should accept collaboration to rapidly and effectively build up a satisfactory current enemy of emergency circumstance, Keynesian financial approach and productively apply it to decrease the size of the gauge monetary downturn in 2020.

In my nation today (17.3.2020), the Fiscal Strategy Chamber at the national bank, for example, at the National Bank of Poland, brought down the essential loan fees by 0.5 focuses percent. From 1.5 percent at 1.0 percent, it was an adjustment in financing costs following a 5-year time of permanence. Around the same time (17.3.2020), the stock records on the national stock trade rose by a few percent. Dynamic declines after about 14 days. Another decrease in loan costs is impossible considering the productivity of Treasury securities offered to remote speculators. They expect a lot higher financing cost on these instruments gave by a little, creating nation comparative with undifferentiated from instruments for the sheltered position of money related surpluses, for example, bonds given by the State Treasury exceptionally created, portrayed by commonly higher efficiency, creation potential, and capital assets in the budgetary segment. The impact of budgetary market brain science worked; however, it is a transient impact and considered for the most part by investigators utilizing specialized examination and, to a lesser degree, a crucial examination. Be that as it may, the significance of the national bank financing cost decrease on monetary impacts in the genuine economy over a more drawn out period is increasingly significant. Business and shopper advances in business, while banks have a lot higher loan fees than the financing cost. The national bank also, the hole between financing costs on stores and stores just as credits at business banks is enormous in certain nations and, in this manner, the genuine impact of decreasing loan fees. The national bank can be extremely restricted. Furthermore, in certain nations, business banks are not obliged to bring down their financing costs naturally. At the point when the national bank does it. What's more, after a decrease in financing costs. By the national bank, business banks are bringing down, watching one another, as a major aspect of interbank rivalry, for the most part from the outset financing costs stores and stores, and simply after some time they choose to diminish loan fees on advances and para-acknowledge items, for example, renting, calculating, and so forth to a constrained degree, and so on. A special case to this standard might be the circumstance when a significant piece of the financial area is controlled in a roundabout way by the administration through the Treasury Lion's shareholding in the shareholding of some biggest business banks in a given nation. Then these procedures can be done quicker, for example, through political weight.

Notwithstanding, if remote monetary organizations notice such an enormous effect of approach in monetary procedures, in the activity of the financial framework, in the working of the money related framework, they may survey this issue as high, extra foundational, and political hazard. Then remote money related foundations, including universally working banks and speculation assets, may leave proceeding with venture exercises in this kind of nation. In a situation where an outside budgetary foundation gave a substantial inflow of monetary funding to household protection showcases and was responsible for a significant part of the capitalization of the entire stock trading advertisement. The constructive mental outcomes of the national bank's loan fee cuts in the more drawn out term may, sadly, no longer work in the genuine economy. [...] Business people know this and along these lines lower financing costs. By 0.5 focuses percent. In this kind of circumstance, it will have little impact in the genuine economy as an expert turn of events against the emergency interventionist instrument of fiscal approach (and from a more extensive perspective additionally of monetary arrangement in case of deficient autonomy of the national bank from the administration). Then again, if the national bank, as a component of the interventionist fiscal arrangement, embraces the acquisition of treasury protections to improve liquidity likewise in the open monetary framework, then it can work "mentally" and has an extremely significant ace advancement drive if extra cash is extremely significant for business visionaries for speculation advancement. Be that as it may, in the circumstance of danger, a solid decrease in financial development and downturn, such instruments of gentle money related arrangement might be justified, as most undertakings no longer consider the improvement of the organization and the usage of ensuing venture ventures, settle on choices for keeping up liquidity and maintaining a strategic distance from budgetary insolvency. In such a circumstance, augmenting and extending the size of mellow money related arrangements might be justified if it doesn't prompt a solid ascent in expansion and, as an outcome, the danger of expanded swelling, which could be a prologue to another kind of monetary emergency. This hazard might be enormous without the genuine autonomy of the national bank.

In my nation, just because, the national bank intends to purchase Treasury securities for a huge scope with the goal that their financing cost doesn't increment significantly, for example as an instrument of keeping up liquidity in the open money related framework in a circumstance where there is a deficiency of outside financial specialists to roll recently gave securities arrangement. Along these lines, Poland will stay away from the danger of an emergency out in the open funds as per a model known from the nations of southern Europe, in which this sort of emergency has happened since pre-winter 2008 when the worldwide budgetary emergency showed up. This potential interventionist money related strategy instrument, comprising in the acquisition of Treasury securities from the optional market by the national bank in Poland, was presented as an extra instrument of monetary framework security after the presence of the worldwide budgetary emergency in 2008. This interventionist instrument at the national bank's removal has been working for quite a long while in a few different nations, including the biggest economies of the Somewhat English Saxon budgetary framework, and was utilized broadly in those nations after the worldwide money related emergency in fall 2008. In Poland, in any case, so far, the National Bank of Poland has not utilized this choice as a major aspect of facilitated exercises with spending arrangement oversaw by the administration through focal organizations of the state's open fund framework.

Nonetheless, at present, the circumstance is uncommon. Amazingly great danger of losing money related liquidity in the state's open account framework, because a significant piece of all-around working outside financial specialists, including speculation banks and venture reserves, maintain a strategic distance from protections gave in nations that are little economies, creating economies portrayed by raised credit and speculation hazard. It is currently conceivable to apply this interventionist instrument for an enormous scope because the dynamic groups of the European Association in this specific circumstance have annulled the commitment for EU part states to apply the brilliant principle of state accounts, for example, keeping up a spending shortfall of up to 3%. Gross domestic product. Given this unique circumstance, the possibility of a liquidity emergency in the framework of the state accounts, the issue of national bank autonomy is losing significance, offering route to the issue of the expanded facilitated interventionist, hostile to the emergency exercises of the financial strategy and a softened one, giving liquidity to the state's budgetary framework and business banks for money related arrangement of the bank focal.

At present (mid-Walk 2020), capital markets keep on ruling feelings, for example, the brain science of monetary markets over the cool, crucial examination. Because of the expanding size of human contamination with Coronavirus SARS-Cov-2 causing COVID-19 malady, the danger of further disease increments quickly. Since the quantity of coronavirus contaminations is as yet rising quickly in numerous nations, the effect of the scourge on the economy will be exceptionally high on the worldwide monetary development rate. The World Exchange Association has declared that a developing plague in numerous nations, on practically all mainland's, may as of now be alluded to as a coronavirus pandemic. The degree of vulnerability to concerning the size of the negative effect on monetary procedures is extremely high. There are no exact estimates that can be utilized to quantify the degree of effect of a developing pandemic on the size of the anticipated decrease in monetary development in the worldwide economy and also in individual nation's economies. It is just sure that this effect will be enormous. Many vehicles and traveler organizations will fail. Numerous inns, organizations offering administrations identified with the travel industry, cooking administrations, diversion administrations, film, and so on will have genuine budgetary issues in the coming many months. In numerous nations, governments are propelling enemies of emergency monetary help programs for undertakings that are now detailing declining deals incomes and have money related issues because of the improvement of the coronavirus pandemic. In numerous nations, be that as it may, the conceivable outcomes of against emergency monetary approach of offering low-intrigue advances or non-repayable awards to undertakings are restricted in light of the fact that, in numerous nations, after the past worldwide money related emergency of 2008, there are still high open obligations charged to open funds. Therefore, with respect to an extending coronavirus pandemic over the next few weeks or months, the size of the negative impacts of coronavirus on the global economy could increase significantly. It's surprising that no one can precisely determine the size of such negative impacts. The powerlessness in quantifying new hazard classes causes an elevated level of vulnerability. . Additionally, vulnerability applies to venture choices taken by speculators and investors working on budgetary markets, fundamentally capital markets, including protections markets. For three weeks at this point, there has been a stock accident on the biggest and numerous littler stock trades, a frenzy offer of offers. The cost of a barrel of oil is additionally falling. Value and oil costs are, as of now, the most minimal since the past worldwide budgetary emergency. The issue is deteriorating quickly. The size of stock value decreases on stock trades may recommend a solid break in the upward patterns in earlier years and may mean a change to a long haul, going on for a long time or perhaps numerous years descending pattern, a droop in the valuation of protections and numerous different resources esteemed on capital markets. Therefore, the accompanying inquiry gets applicable: Can a coronavirus pandemic trigger a worldwide monetary emergency in 2020, including a downturn enduring weeks or months in numerous nations?

Because of the expanding size of human leaf contamination with coronavirus SARS-Cov-2 causing COVID-19 sickness, the multi-faceted effect of plague improvement on the economy, remembering the circumstance for money related markets, is expanding. In this manner, I propose a conversation on the accompanying point:

Effect of coronavirus on financial matters, including monetary development rate and money related markets.

In start of Walk 2020, the size of sharp abatements in the valuation of protections shares on the stock trades and a fall in the cost for a barrel of oil gets the qualities of a stock accident. Moreover, there is a significant decrease in the creation of numerous items extends made in China, and so forth. The Swiss franc is ascending against a portion of the other financially increasingly well-known monetary forms. Incomes and benefits in the travel industry segment are falling emphatically in numerous nations. Can this circumstance be deciphered as far as signs proposing the chance of another worldwide financial emergency in 2020? Could a solid auction of stock costs on stock trades despite everything toward the end in the next days? Could this mean an adjustment in the drawn-out long haul upward pattern to a descending pattern and the bust on the securities exchanges that went on for a long time?

In this association, the accompanying further significant inquiry emerges: What against emergency Keynesian financial strategy should legislatures of nations create to neutralize the developing size of the monetary downturn, remembering the significant lessening towards orders for different item goes, crude materials, decline underway, potential fast increment in joblessness, a reduction in salary and utilization? What instruments of enterprise initiation ought to be created as a component of hostile to an emergency financial arrangement? Right now, an especially significant issue to be settled is the response to the inquiry: Can a solid auction of stock costs accomplishing the qualities of a securities exchange crash like that of the financial exchange crash.

TODAY'S AMERICA: A LAND OF BROKEN FAMILIES AND FEW PROSPECTS

Various things can influence kid advancement/conduct, yet a major factor might be guardians. Contingent upon the seriousness of a messed up home, the parent's relationship with one another, just as their youngsters, can influence how their kids carry on and may even create. It does not mean that a parent's separation can cause it so that a kid can never climb steps or bounce on one foot, but it can make it more difficult for kids to develop social abilities and even interfere with their accomplishments. The division of their folks, depending on a child's age, can cause outrageous pressure, and even despondency, in the most pessimistic scenario. Nonetheless, keeping the parent's hitched probably won't be in the wellbeing either, depending on the family's circumstance. As far as I can tell of originating from a messed up home, I have never experienced formative or conduct issues.

Nonetheless, that may be attributed to my folks staying in a similar house after the separation, the age at which my parents were separated, and also the relationship I had with each of my parents, just as they had with each other. Guardians affect their kids, wedded or not. Broken homes significantly affect young people and can proceed for the duration of their lives.

In order to see how a messed up home affects kid advancement/conduct, it is important to see how youngsters ought to create/act typically. Although a kid may carry on and create at their own rate, there are rules for a youngster's turn of events, just like behavior, with regards to their psychological capacity. The above picture shows the formative abilities that a youngster ought to have at the given ages, a considerable lot of which have to do with the engine and social aptitudes. As found in the outline, youngsters need to create things they can do to assist them with doing straightforward errands, such as brushing their teeth and strolling heel to toe. Creating engine abilities will cause a kid to turn out to be progressively free, perceiving how they will be moving and getting a handle on things all alone. So this is an easy decision: kids need to create engine abilities. However, something else a kid needs to grow, additionally appeared by the diagram, is social aptitudes. This would incorporate naming things and getting words. Barbara Solomon, a social specialist with a Four-year education in science qualification in brain research and a Ph.D. from the College of Southern California, remarks on how "absence of social capacities could flag a clinical or formative issue" (Solomon, 2004). So not exclusively are an absence of engine aptitudes an issue at a young age; however, so are social abilities.

In conclusion, there are three kinds of conduct that guardians ought to comprehend with regards to their kids. To begin with, there is conduct that is endorsed. This incorporates conduct, for example, being caring to others, being understanding, and tuning in to other people. The second kind of conduct is one that isn't needed consistently; however, it is endured. This conduct can be brought about by the kid being focused or debilitated and is comprehended in setting, and, contingent upon the family, different sorts of conduct are endured. The last kind of conduct is one that ought not to go on without serious consequences. This sort can be irksome for a kid's scholarly turn of events and may even reason damage to the "physical, enthusiastic, or social prosperity of the kid" (Ordinary Youngster Conduct, 2015). This sort of conduct can also be brought on by the parent, depending upon how they act inwardly. Youngsters may begin to duplicate their parent's conduct due to how intently they tail them for the ordinary passionate responses of society. This may become problematic, depending on whether the parent is forceful and following up on outrage. For this situation, when a kid begins to mirror their parent, they build up the third kind of conduct.

An examination to show psychological testing in young people has appeared in the picture above. This examination was finished by Anna Sanz-de-Galdeano and Daniela Vuri alongside IZA. The Establishment for the Investigation of Work, in 2004. This was an examination to check whether the subjective advancement of young people were changed depending on the reality of their present family circumstance. This information shows the families that are unblemished has a higher psychological capacity than families that are not flawless. In any case, the examination that was additionally directed indicated similar youngsters having lower psychological capacity before their folks got separated. The examination in this investigation shows that youngster's subjective capacity won't decline, yet that doesn't utter a word about the impact on more youthful kids. This investigation reasons that in the short run, teenagers with separated from families may have a lower psychological capacity, regardless of whether they have a lower subjective capacity before their folks are separated. Over the long haul, this is the equivalent. This examination is reliable with was Cherlin et al. (1995) stated, similar to the planning of parental separation, the age that separation happens "(ages 7 to 11 versus ages 11 to 16) in a kid's life doesn't have any effect for youthful grown-up results" (Sanz-de-Galdeano and Vuri, 2004). So whether a kid is more youthful versus more established when their folks separate, that doesn't mean it will influence them as a grown-up: the youngster will have the equivalent subjective capacity before separate, as appeared in this investigation, just as after the separation.

Another investigation recommends that a parent has a significant result on their kid's passionate turn of events. Being truly present may not be sufficient for a youngster, and the only important thing is their parent's enthusiastic connection to them (Volling referred to in Moges and Weber, 2014). If the parent isn't genuinely associated with their kid, "the youngster will battle to figure out how to direct his feelings and cooperate with others fittingly" (Moges and Weber, 2014). With my involvement in separate, my mom was genuinely there. However, she was never sincerely there. I would state that I experienced sporadic feelings when it went to my mom. Now and again, I would be extremely content with her since she was there with me. Different occasions, and maybe more often than not, I was furious with her on account of how little she appeared to think about my life. Since I was so negative towards my mom's negative demeanor, it shows this can "often

[lead] to considerably increasingly social issues" (Moges and Weber, 2014). This is hazardous when bringing up a kid to turn into a balanced grown-up because it might prompt further difficulties while interfacing with others typically. There is nobody approach to raise a superbly composed kid, yet guardians can avoid potential risks when dealing with them inwardly. It is critical to give them "steady condition, positive input, good examples of sound conduct and connections, and somebody to converse with about their passionate responses to their encounters" (Morges and Weber, 2014). This will guarantee that the kid will be okay sincerely when growing up, and not having any issues with regards to directing feelings and connecting with others.

An assessment in 1971 demonstrated 60 isolated from families nearby 131 children. Following five years, 66% of the youths "were clinically disheartened, were doing ineffectually in school, experienced issues taking care of connections, [and] experienced relentless issues, for instance, rest aggravations" (Amato, 2005). As maintained by the assessment, these youths may have started acting compelling and "partaking in tormenting conduct, the two of which can unfavorably impact peer associations" (Green). Regardless, another assessment, done in 1970, demonstrated how the following two years of their parent's division, preschoolers didn't show energetic and social issues as they did the earlier year. So why does one social affair of children show more genuine reactions than the other get-together? The fitting reaction is this: ask about shows that the second most defenseless assembling to isolate is energetic youngsters, addressed by the get-together of children in the examination done in 1971 (Blakeslee and Wallerstein,

2006). The chief get-together to be the most impacted by discrete are little children before they enter school. This way, for this circumstance, preschoolers won't be as affected as much as energetic youngsters would. At this age, energetic youngsters are being pushed fairly into the world, thinking about future vocations, school, sports and clubs, nostalgic associations, and the summary goes on. With the whole of this, the division may add to the summary to make it progressively upsetting for the youth, realizing enthusiastic and direct issues. In any case, if a parent didn't require a detachment because of this clarification, the outcome most likely won't be too aspected as one would presume. If a child's parent is constantly involved, this will add more concern to the family and may really hurt an adolescent. As already communicated, the gatekeepers have something to do with how a child is deep down. A child will, in like manner, see how their people associate and their copy direct, similarly as pessimistic imperativeness (Moges and Weber, 2014). Engaging gatekeepers that stay together, taking into account their child may end up achieving more wickedness than none. Broken homes may not hurt a youth developmentally or mentally yet rather may incorporate a significant activity inside their guidance, direct, social aptitudes, and eager capacities depending upon their age.

Appeared differently concerning a youth being isolated from family. This child is brought into the world outside of marriage or simply has one parent may "show up at adulthood with less guidance, winless compensation, ... will undoubtedly have a nonmarital birth, ... and report symptoms of wretchedness progressively" than an isolated child would

(Amato, 2005). The single parent is in like manner at a disaster financially, making it more difficult to afford their child things for a school they ought to succeed. Concerning guidance, youths with broken homes may experience nonattendance of academic progression. This may "originate from different segments, recalling insecurity for the home condition, insufficient.

It is difficult to identify what causes a kid to act in a specific way, or do things the way that they do. In any case, it has appeared again and again through research that messed up homes influence kids, contingent upon their age passionate stance with their folks, more than wedded families do. There will never be a way that a kid can be raised, and because one might be raised in a messed up home doesn't mean they will experience the ill effects of melancholy or enthusiastic issues. Broken homes won't really ruin a youngster's turn of events or subjective capacity. Nonetheless, it might cause an issue with their training or conduct. By and large, a solitary parent or separated from guardians acquire less cash than a married family does, making it harder to seek after things that their kids may require for training or different needs, bringing about additional issues later on. It is significant for families to see how to give a steady and safe home for youngsters to experience childhood in to constrain issues, for example, these. Over the long haul, a kid that experiences childhood in a protected domain will develop into a balanced grown-up and will pay off in the ages to come.

WHAT FUTURE DIFFICULTIES WILL ORIGINATORS FACE?

There are different sorts of business visionaries doing different kinds of things, so it's difficult to sum up, yet it begins with having a convincing item. Then how would you collect a group to take that thought and put it without hesitation and scale it into a significant manageable business?

I think there are additionally going to be someone of a kind and, to some degree, complex difficulties for this next flood of business people who are changing medicinal services or instruction. That will require a higher level of tirelessness. It will likewise require building coalitions with different organizations or foundations, just as connecting on the arrangement side with the government. The open doors are significant, yet it will require a different range of abilities. A few things that are imperative to organizations - like items, individuals, and enthusiasm - will continue as before. Some new things- - organizations, arrangement, constancy - will turn out to be progressively significant too.

The model in this last wave- - especially for the organizations concentrated on applications - was, you dispatch your application, and inside a year, you'd either get a ton of footing or you wouldn't. If you got footing, you'd expand on that. If you didn't, you'd accomplish something different. You got a close to momentary market response. In this next wave, it will take more time to truly have sway.

Why do you think there will be increasingly mind-boggling difficulties? Why not more applications?

There will be more applications. A portion of that will proceed. So if you need to think of another application, you can keep on concentrating on that. What's more, numerous individuals will. In any case, I believe another gathering of organizations and developments will begin rising, which requires a different system.

You've said before that business people of things to come would be less ready to go only it. Why?

There are absolutely some who might go only it. Be that as it may, the business enterprise is a group activity. One individual can do just to such an extent. To truly have a broad effect, it boils down to how you manufacture the group around you to get the influence and impact at the scale that you need.

Despite the fact that there were some notorious business people, including Steve Employments, who deservedly got a great deal of consideration, the genuine discoveries occur through groups. That has been the situation for a large portion of the huge pioneering examples of overcoming adversity, and I figure it will be considerably more the case for this next influx of organizations. The way toward changing how children learn in school is confused and multifaceted. You can't simply sit at your PC and get it going. That will require a group.

What's your best guide for future business visionaries?

Ensure you're identifying a major issue that should be settled or an open door that should be seized- - and put it all on the line. I don't mean any lack of respect to business visionaries who decide to accomplish something smaller, yet I'd urge individuals to swing for the wall. Those are harder issues; however, I believe they're progressively significant issues and the issues that make more chances. What's more, at last, you can fabricate a significant business with the possibility to positively affect a huge number of individuals' lives.

Take a more drawn out term, worked to-last view. Also, perceive that you can't go only it, that you have to fabricate a group and key organizations. If you do that effectively, you can fabricate an extraordinary organization you can be pleased with, and one that powerfully affects society.

Constant illness is driving the expense of social insurance in America.

As indicated by the Habitats for Illness Control and Anticipation (CDC), medications for ceaseless maladies make up 86 percent of the nation's human services costs. Dr. Murthy talked about how the government can assume a job in controlling these pestilences—going from stoutness to diabetes—with successful guidelines of the business and advancing sound lifestyles the nation over.

We have to gather bits of knowledge from our information with the goal that we can grow increasingly powerful, and understanding focused wellbeing frameworks.

Holmberg noticed that human services suppliers and back up plans like Highmark Wellbeing could utilize information to make frameworks that treat patients adequately. Ms. Verma featured how the CMS has recently patched up its medication spending dashboard by including more information remedies' expenses. By making importance out of the bounty of data that as of now exists, both people in general and private segments are building a framework that works for the regular shopper.

Coordinated effort—not division—is fundamental to making a sound future for all Americans.

All features of the business—from pharmaceuticals to suppliers, to guarantors, to controllers—are profoundly associated. Both Dr. Murthy and Mr. Holmberg concurred that cooperation over the medicinal services industry is critical to tending to a portion of our nation's most squeezing social insurance challenges.

www.ingramcontent.com/pod-product-compliance
Lightning Source LLC
Chambersburg PA
CBHW071411210526
45465CB00001B/337